PEDDLERS
and PRINCES

PEDDLERS
and PRINCES

*Social Change and Economic Modernization
in Two Indonesian Towns*

Clifford Geertz

THE UNIVERSITY OF CHICAGO PRESS

CHICAGO AND LONDON

THE UNIVERSITY OF CHICAGO PRESS, CHICAGO 60637
The University of Chicago Press, Ltd., London

Published 1963
Printed and bound by CPI Group (UK) Ltd, Croydon, CR0 4YY
93 92 91   11 10 9

ISBN: 978-0-226-28514-6 (hardback); ISBN: 978-0-226-28514-6 (paperback)

Library of Congress Catalog Card Number: 63-18844

To the Memory of Donald Fagg

Acknowledgments

The following study is based on two separate field trips to Indonesia. The first was to Java, as part of the "Modjokuto Project" sponsored by the Ford Foundation under the auspices of the Center for International Studies of the Massachusetts Institute of Technology, and took place in 1952–54. The second, also under the auspices of the MIT Center but sponsored by the Rockefeller Foundation, was to Bali in 1957–58, during which period a short return visit to the Java research site was also made. I am grateful to my colleagues on the Modjokuto Project — Alice Dewey, Donald Fagg, Hildred Geertz, Rufus Hendon, Edward Ryan and Robert Jay — as well as to Douglas Oliver, who planned the project, and Max Millikan, Director of the Center, for their support and friendship throughout. With respect to the Bali trip, Everett Hagen provided both intellectual and material assistance for which I am most grateful, while discussions with other members of the Center — especially Benjamin Higgins, Guy Pauker, and Douglas Pauuw — were most helpful in formulating my study and bringing it to completion.

The book was written during my fellowship at the Center for Advanced Study in the Behavioral Sciences in 1958–59 and rewritten while a member of the Committee for the Comparative Study of New Nations at the University of Chicago; and to both of these estimable institutions, the second modeled on the first, I am most indebted, as well as to various of their members who read and criticized parts of the work.

In the sequel I have made no attempt to make corrections for occurrences which have taken place in Indonesia since I left four years ago. Thus references to "now," "today," etc. refer to the 1952–59 period, and some corrections would no doubt have to be made if one were to look at these two towns in 1963, the real "now." The disappearance of the Masjumi and Socialist parties and, in fact, of a good deal of the free political combat of the early post-Revolution phase, the supposed removal of the Chinese from small towns, the growing importance of the army are all matters which have no doubt altered the situation to a degree, though precisely how much it is not possible at this distance to say. It is my own feeling, however, that despite the surface noise there has not been very much fundamental socioeconomic change in Indonesia since the Revolution, and the bulk of the descriptions and analyses made below still obtain.

To my wife, my co-worker on both projects, I owe a debt of such dimensions that acknowledgment seems but a vain and meager gesture. I have instead dedicated the book to a friend of both us who was a colleague on our first trip and who died, in the United States, while we were in the midst of our second. It is not, perhaps, the book he would have written; but I think it is the sort of which he would have approved.

Contents

1. Introduction

The introduction of the concept of "take-off" into recent discussions of the process of economic development in non-industrial societies has served two useful functions. First, it has emphasized the discontinuous nature of this process. Second, it has underlined the fact that the characteristic problems facing a national economy change with the phase of the whole process that economy happens to be passing through.[1] By dramatizing the fact that when conditions are right, the transition from stagnancy to sustained growth may be so very rapid as to be explosive, the "take-off" concept has sharpened our awareness that the problems of development are quite different in nations just entering the transition (such as China or, probably, India) than in those (such as Mexico or Turkey) which, having successfully passed through it, are well launched into a phase of steady rise in per capita income. The "quantum jump," "step-function," "industrial revolution" view of economic modernization gives at least some degree of determinate form to what is otherwise but a vague and ill-defined process.

One of the dangers of this approach, however, is that it is likely

[1] See W. W. Rostow, *The Stages of Economic Growth* (Cambridge: Cambridge University Press, 1960).

to lead us to employ per capita income as an exclusive index of the process of economic development and in so doing cause us to focus our attention on those points in the process where the changes are most dramatic. In one sense, of course, increasing per capita income *is* economic growth, not a mere index of it; but in another, it is clear that such increases are but one highly visible resultant of a complex process which they reflect in only a broad and imprecise fashion, so that a simple identification of the pattern of change in per capita income with the pattern of social change which produces it is highly misleading. Though it may be true that, as an economic process, development is a dramatic, revolutionary change, as a broadly social process it fairly clearly is not. What looks like a quantum jump from a specifically economic point of view is, from a generally social one, merely the final expression in economic terms of a process which has been building up gradually over an extended period of time.

This becomes particularly apparent when one comes to consider countries which have not yet entered the take-off phase but seem reasonably likely to do so in the not-too-distant future. In such countries, per capita income may be increasing little if at all; in some cases it may even be dropping. Yet it is difficult to put aside the impression that fundamental social and cultural changes which may ultimately pave the way for rapid economic growth are occurring. Certainly, it has become more and more apparent that Tokugawa Japan, pre-1917 Russia, and the England of 1750 were not merely periods of quiet, unchanging stability before a sudden cataclysm of economic revolution, but rather periods of widespread intellectual and social ferment in which crucial social relationships and cultural values were being altered in such a way as to allow an eventual large-scale reorganization of productive activities. It is at least possible that by the time take-off occurs a great proportion of the social transformations we associate with industrialism are, in the typical case, well under way. The sudden burst of growth in income and investment a nation's economy characteristically shows during the first years of its modernization is in part the result of a concentration on economic changes made possible by the fact that certain broader and more fundamental changes have already been effected, so that creative energies can now be channeled to more directly productive ends.

Indonesia is now, by all the signs and portents, in the midst of such a pretake-off period. The years since 1945, and in fact since about 1920, have seen the beginnings of a fundamental transformation in social values and institutions toward patterns we generally associate with a developed economy, even though actual progress toward the creation of such an economy has been slight and sporadic at best. Alterations in the system of social stratification, in world view and ethos, in political and economic organization, in education, and even in family structure have occurred over a wide section of the society. Many of the changes — the commercialization of agriculture, the formation of non-familial business concerns, the heightened prestige of technical skills vis-à-vis religious and aesthetic ones — which more or less immediately preceded take-off in the West have also begun to appear, and industrialization, in quite explicit terms, has become one of the primary political goals of the nation as a whole.

Yet that all these changes will finally add up to take-off is far from certain. It is clearly possible for development to misfire at any stage, even the initial one. Levy has shown, for example, how many of the social changes prerequisite to industrialization took place in China toward the end of the Ching dynasty — most notably the dissolution of the extended family system — without the promised economic growth following:

For the last five decades or more China has been a sort of no man's land with regard to modernization. It has bits and parts of it, but it has not achieved any considerable level of industrialization. It also has not been able to regain a stable version of the "traditional" society it once had.[2]

Except that the time span is shorter, this description fits contemporary Indonesia, most particularly Java, as well as it does China.

[2] M. J. Levy, "Contrasting Factors in the Modernization of China and Japan," in S. Kuznets et al (eds.), *Economic Growth: Brazil, India, Japan* (Durham, N.C.: Duke University Press, 1955), pp. 496–536.

The transition to a modern society has begun; whether — or perhaps better, when — it will be completed is far from certain.

In such a pretake-off society, where traditional equilibrium has been irrevocably lost but the more dynamic equilibrium of an industrial society has not yet been attained, the investigation of the prospects for development breaks down into two fairly separable analytical tasks. First, there is the task of discerning the changes toward modernization which are in fact taking place. What social and cultural transformations are under way which seem, on a comparative and theoretical basis, likely to facilitate development? Second, there is what we might call the "critical mass" problem: the task of estimating the stage these various changes must reach and the interrelations between them which must obtain before take-off will in fact occur. What is the constellation of social and cultural forces which must be realized for development to start and a breakout from the no man's land of neither traditional nor modern be achieved? We need both to isolate the various processes ingredient in modernization and to consider when and how these processes add up to take-off in economic terms.

In general, anthropologists have concentrated their attention on the first of these analytical tasks, economists on the second. The method of anthropology — intensive, first-hand field study of small social units within the larger society — means that its primary contribution to the understanding of economic development must inevitably lie in a relatively microscopic and circumstantial analysis of a wide range of social processes as they appear in concrete form in this village, or that town, or the other social class; the theoretical framework of the economist almost as inevitably trains his interest on the society as a whole and on the aggregate implications for the entire economy of the processes the anthropologist studies in miniature. One result of this division of labor has been that anthropological studies of development have tended to consist of a set of more or less disconnected examples of the various social forces which "somehow" play a part in development with little or no indication as to how they play this part or how they effect the over-all functioning of the economy; economic studies of development tend to consist of general statements about the implications of various sorts of relationships among technically defined aggregate economic variables for growth, with little or no indication of how the social forces determining the value of these variables can be expected to behave. On the one hand you have a sociological eclecticism stressing gradualism, on the other an economic formalism stressing revolution.

Although this book follows in the anthropological tradition in attempting to evaluate Indonesia's development prospects by focusing on concrete examples of social change found in two Indonesian towns, it is clear that a really effective theory of economic growth will appear only when the social process and take-off approaches are joined in a single framework of analysis, when the relationships between the broad changes in social stratification, or political structure, or cultural values which facilitate growth, and the specific changes in levels of saving and investment we hold to cause it can be related one to another. Such an ideal is not to be achieved by one definitive study, but rather will be realized slowly as anthropologists gradually give a more unambiguous interpretation of their findings in terms of general theoretical problems and economists gradually give sociological content to their aggregate models. Like two tunnel builders working on opposite sides of the same mountain, each must dig in his own spot with his own tools and approach each other only step by step. But if they are eventually to meet in the middle and so construct a single tunnel, each must try, in the meantime, to orient his own work to that of the other.

Our description of the processes of socioeconomic change now taking place in two towns, one Javanese and one Balinese, will include a discussion of some of the implications of these changes for a general analysis of Indonesian take-off prospects. More specifically, we shall both isolate the major dynamics of economic growth in these two towns and seek to determine how a detailed knowledge of such particular, circumscribed, and seemingly parochial social forces contributes to the formulation of over-all developmental policies and programs. To do so is to confront the problem of the relation between local and national, between gradual and sudden, and between social and economic change directly and to move, part way at least, toward an eventual reconciliation of the economist's and the anthropologist's way of looking at development.

2. Two Indonesian Towns

The two towns which we shall compare are Modjokuto, in eastern central Java, and Tabanan, in southwest Bali. Modjokuto, which lies at the eastern edge of the great semicircular Brantas river valley some one hundred miles south of its mouth at Surabaja, Indonesia's third seaport, is typical of the drab, overcrowded, busily commercial little crossroads towns which occur every fifteen or twenty miles along the main thoroughfares of the central Java rice plains; Tabanan, about twenty miles west of Den Pasar, the capital of Bali, is the former seat of a Balinese royal court and a traditional center of art and politics. Both are located in fertile, heavily populated, irrigated rice regions, of which they are the administrative, commercial, and educational capitals; both provide the main local arena for cultural contact between "East" and "West," "traditional" and "modern," and "local" and "national"; and both show clear evidences that they are undergoing fundamental social, political, and economic changes. Though culturally diverse and displaying certain important differences in social structure, the two towns stem from a common historical tradition, represent approximately the same level of organizational complexity, and are members of a single national polity and economy. It is this similarity amid difference which gives them their peculiar value for the analysis of Indonesian development.

MODJOKUTO: A JAVANESE MARKET TOWN

Modjokuto looks like any of a hundred other small Javanese towns: a banyan tree with a Hindu statue at its foot in the public square; a cluster of government offices centered around the District Officer's house with its traditional deep veranda and broad front yard; a line of open-fronted, awning-shaded Chinese stores and warehouses; a large, open market place with rusted tin sheds and wooded stalls; a mosque, gleaming a painful white in the tropical sun; and hundreds of small bamboo-walled, dirt-floor houses crowded helter-skelter onto the large blocks formed by the street grid. There are a motion picture theater, two small hospitals, a government pawnshop, a couple of dozen elementary and secondary schools, a bus depot, and a narrow-gauge railway with station, repair shop, and miniature wood-burning locomotives which look like fanciful Victorian toys. Set amid the rice fields which square off the flat countryside into a giant checkerboard, the town, only about two square kilometers in area, seems to amount to hardly more than the literal meaning ("stopping place") of its (real) name.

But 24,000 people — 2,000 of them Chinese — live here, and a great deal goes on. The district and subdistrict offices, assisted by such special agencies as the agricultural extension, irrigation, and state police offices, administer the affairs of the national state for some 250,000 and 85,000 people, spread over 167 and 30 square miles respectively.[1] The market forms the hub of a far-flung and intensively active trade network through which a fabulous variety of goods flow and from which probably a majority of the town population in one way or another draws its living. Even today, when government devices designed to obstruct it are invented almost daily, the Chinese trade in both the export of cash crops

---

[1] For a general description of the town and surrounding area see C. Geertz, *The Social Context of Economic Change: An Indonesian Case Study* (Cambridge, Mass.: Center for International Studies, Massachusetts Institute of Technology, 1956 [dittoed]). For the rural area in particular see R. Jay, "Local Government in Rural Central Java," *Far Eastern Quarterly*, XV, No. 2 (Feb. 1956), 215–27.

and the import of manufactured goods remains quite sizable. There is an enormous elaboration of modern nationalist political life, with a great many parties, labor unions, youth groups, women's clubs, religious associations, and the like engaged in a continual struggle for power which mirrors the similar nation-wide struggle centered in Djakarta. And there are probably over 2,000 students in the various schools which range from six-grade elementary schools, through technical trade schools, privately owned junior high schools, and government teachers' schools. If the physical picture is one of a rather tired shabbiness, the social picture is almost one of hyperactivity.

Modjokuto comes by this hyperactivity naturally. Founded only toward the latter half of the nineteenth century, in what was then one of the less densely populated areas of Central Java, it became by 1925 a rapidly expanding boom town as the result of Dutch activities in large-scale commercial agriculture, most particularly in cane sugar, in the surrounding countryside.[2] By that date there were ten sugar mills, three tapioca mills, and two sisal mills within a twenty-mile radius of the town. In the same area Dutch concerns held about 20,000 acres of plantation land on long leases from the Netherlands East Indies Government, and about a quarter of the peasant-owned riceland immediately around the town was being rented yearly for sugar growing by these concerns.[3] By this time (1925) the railway had seven branch lines to the various mills, and the volume of freight it carried rose 4,000 per cent between 1900 and 1929. Commerce of all kinds boomed, even among the Indonesian population. The textile, tobacco, and salted fish trades expanded rapidly. Restaurants, hardware stores, and drug stores sprang up. Immigration, particularly of Chinese, spurted, and the annual rate of population increase went well over 2 per cent. More and more peasants found themselves working seasonally as plantation coo-

[2] For details see Geertz, *op. cit.* pp. 29 ff. The first plantation appeared in 1875.

[3] The comparable figure for Java as a whole at this time was 6 per cent, indicating the degree to which Modjokuto may properly be referred to as a "sugar area." G. H. Van der Kolff, "An Economic Case Study: Sugar and Welfare in Java" in P. Ruopp (ed.), *Approaches to Community Development* (The Hague and Bandung: W. Van Hoeve, 1953), pp. 188–206.

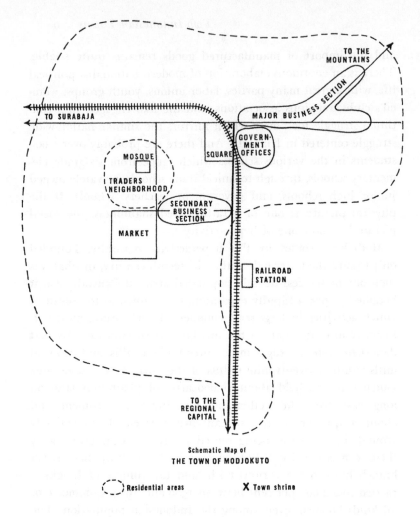

TO THE
MOUNTAINS

TO SURABAJA

MAJOR BUSINESS SECTION

MOSQUE

TRADERS
NEIGHBORHOOD

GOVERN-
MENT
OFFICES

SQUARE

SECONDARY
BUSINESS
SECTION

MARKET

RAILROAD
STATION

TO THE
REGIONAL
CAPITAL

Schematic Map of
THE TOWN OF MODJOKUTO

Residential areas   X Town shrine

lies, landlessness increased, and a class of slightly richer peasants
emerged in the villages, often acting as land and labor contrac-
tors to the mills on the side. In the mills, technical jobs for Indonesians, at least at the lower levels, became more and more numerous, while the growth of the railroad and the plantations also
provided more manual labor jobs. By the time all this expansion
fell apart in the crash of the thirties, which was particularly severe
in Java, the urbanization of Modjokuto had been greatly advanced, and the town had become a thriving center of trade, transport, and nationalist political activity.

After the crash — by 1934 NEI sugar production was only about a fifth of what it had been in 1931 — the generally commercial orientation of the town was too far advanced to be reversed. Though the general level of living fell noticeably, a turn to dry season cash crops (maize, soyabean, cassava), mainly financed by Chinese moneylenders, partially replaced sugar as a source of cash income for the peasantry, few of whom were now able to hold on to much more than an acre or two of land. The market was flooded by hundreds of small-scale traders eking out a marginal living where before a few large-scale merchants had made a handsome one. A certain amount of insubstantial and fitfully operating putting-out, cottage, and small factory industry — garment-making, cigarettes, charcoal — appeared in the town and the villages immediately around it. The last days of the colonial regime and the Japanese occupation which followed it were periods of retrenchment for Modjokuto, but not of an actual change of direction as far as development was concerned. The decrease in opportunities for commercial profit led to an overcrowding of those which remained, so that although the town suffered a loss in income it experienced, if anything, an intensification rather than a slowing-down of economic activity. No retreat to traditional subsistence agriculture, village craft work, and highly localized part-time peddling was possible, and the over-all trend toward the conversion of the bulk of Modjokuto's citizens into small-scale businessmen has continued into the postwar period.

The evolution of Modjokuto's social structure also reflects this general trend toward a market-centered society. Until the mid-thirties, the town, like almost all small Javanese towns of this period, was composed of four main groups: the gentry (*prijaji*), consisting of government civil servants plus some of the more higher status white-collar workers from the mills; the traders (*wong dagang*), who were dealers, often fairly substantial ones, in cloth, tobacco, hardware, and so on; the "little people" (*wong tjilik*), consisting of landless laborers, small-scale peasants, and marginal craftsmen (carpenters, bricklayers); and the Chinese (*wong tjina*). The Chinese, almost without exception, were traders and so in broad terms belonged to the *wong dagang* group; but in fact they stood largely outside the Javanese social system altogether, forming a self-contained minority in a society to which, despite some degree of acculturation, they remained essentially foreign.

The gentry, who made up the cultural and political elite of the town, were rather less numerous in Modjokuto than in most contemporary towns of equal size, for Modjokuto was only a district capital where most of the towns otherwise comparable were regency capitals and, consequently, had a very much larger contingent of civil servants.[4] Thus the impact upon the town as a whole of the etiquette and the art-centered, heavily Hinduized, court-oriented style of life affected by these aristocrats turned bureaucrats was rather less intense than elsewhere and the domination of their somewhat over-civilized "high society" less stupefying.

But although the civil servant corps was smaller than normal for a town of Modjokuto's dimensions, the commercial, trader class was, as a secondary effect of the plantation economy, a good deal larger than normal. The leading figures of this group, the large-scale textile, tobacco, and hardware merchants, were strongly pious Moslems (some of them actually of Arab descent), migrants from Java's north coast, for centuries the center of Javanese commercial life and Islamic learning. Thrifty, industrious, and pious, they gave to the town an almost Levantine tone, infusing it with the atmosphere of the bazaar. And their economic organization became so highly developed that for a few years they threatened to capture the bulk of the local trade from the Chinese.

Segregating themselves according to point of origin, these highly professional small businessmen formed well-integrated, regionally based groups tending to specialize in a certain branch of trade: men from one area sold bulk textiles, men from another sold ready-made clothes and cigarettes, those from a third, dried fish and spices, those from a fourth, small hardware, etc. Several entrepôt-type stores, the largest of which boasted a clerical staff of four, a Chinese bookkeeper, and a semi-annual billing arrangement with

[4] A regency is the administrative level next higher than a district and is the major center for regional government in most parts of Java. For civil service organization in Java see A. Vandenbosch, *The Dutch East Indies* (3d ed.; Berkeley: University of California Press, 1942).

a Surabaja importer, sold wholesale cloth on credit and provided ox-carts to carry subcontractors, generally peripatetic traders, to markets as far as thirty miles away. Large, well-integrated trade organizations were employed to pool resources, distribute routes, and enforce debts within the groups. Between the groups there was a good deal of acrimonious competition, commercial jealousy, and mutual disrespect based on regional pride. But at the same time they shared a hyperorthodox religious seriousness which set them off as a whole from the rest of the Modjokuto community, and together they developed, in this brief period of prosperity, a fairly highly organized yet simply patterned regional distributive network linking the town to the general Indonesian economy. They also renovated the mosque, initiated the Islamic Reform movement in the town, sparked the first mass-organized nationalist association (*Sarekat Islam*, "The Islamic Union") to appear in Modjokuto, and sponsored the first secondary schools in the area. Despite the greater cultural prestige of the gentry, the traders were, at this time, the leading, certainly the most dynamic, group in the society. (The third group, the "little people" though there were probably more of them than was typical for a town of Modjokuto's dimensions, played a mainly passive role.)

After the depression, the combination of a weakened economy and an overcrowding of the market network with an increasing number of marginal traders sapped the dynamic of the merchant class at the same time as it tended to dissolve the watertight distinctions between gentleman, trader, and proletarian. Originally, the gentry lived clustered around the District Officer's house, their own elegant homes reduced models of his. The merchants had their own quarter between the mosque and the market, a kasbah-like wilderness of narrow stone alleyways and cement houses. And the manual laborers occupied the bamboo shacks crowded together between unpaved side streets. Like the Chinese who lived in the rear of their stores, each group formed a more or less self-contained subcultural group; interaction between members of different groups extended little beyond the minimum necessary for orderly government and a functioning economy. But toward the end of the colonial period these clearly drawn lines began to blur as civil servants on drastically reduced salaries, dismissed mill clerks, and jobless proletarians all sought to keep their heads above water by engaging in part- or full-time trade. The Japanese, by appointing, for reasons of state, some of the Moslem traders to important local governmental posts, forcing many of the traditional civil servants to labor in the fields, and drafting the "little people" into forced labor work gangs by the scores, disturbed the whole structure even more fundamentally. With the emergence in 1945 of runaway inflation, guerrilla-organized military violence and mass migrations to the countryside to escape Dutch control in the town, the process of dislocation of the traditional social structure was further accelerated to the point where the need for new patterns of organization began to be felt fairly keenly.

To a certain extent this need has been met in the years since Independence by the greatly increased importance of the institutional paraphernalia of Indonesian nationalism, although in general terms Modjokuto still suffers quite severely from a lack of effective social forms around which to organize its life. This institutional paraphernalia consists in the main of the four major all-Indonesia political parties — the *Partai Nasional Indonesia* (PNI), or Nationalist; the *Masjumi*, or Modernist Moslem; the *Nahdatul Ulama* (NU) or Orthodox Moslem; and the *Partai Komunis Indonesia* (PKI), or Communist — plus a whole set of organizational appendages. As well as its political organization proper, each party has connected with it, formally or informally, women's clubs, youth and student groups, labor unions, peasant organizations, charitable associations, private schools, religious or philosophical societies, veterans' organizations, savings clubs, and so forth, which serve to bind it to the local social system. Each party with its aggregation of specialized associations provides, therefore, a general framework within which a wide range of social activities can be organized, as well as an over-all ideological rationale to give those activities point and direction. The resultant complex, as much a social movement as a political party proper, is usually referred to as an *aliran*, the Indonesian term for a stream or current; and it is the *alirans* which today form, inadequately and incompletely, the core of Modjokuto social structure, replacing the traditional status groups of the prewar period.

Each *aliran* is headed in Modjokuto by a party directorate, composed, in the main, of the leaders of the various auxiliary organizations within its ideological camp. To a steadily increasing degree, the members of these directorates — less than a hundred men in all — form the town's "new men of power," an as yet heterogeneous and unconsolidated local elite. Many of the central policy-determining functions of local government are today executed not as traditionally by the civil service, but rather through the agency of a great number of specialized *ad hoc* committees — an Independence Day committee, a (government) rice-buying committee, a veterans' affairs committee — appointed by the District or Subdistrict Officer in such a way as to include representatives from the leadership of each *aliran*. In such an irregular system, the District or Subdistrict Officer himself comes to act more as a much harassed referee between bitterly opposed factions than as the arbitrary and aloof local potentate he was in the prewar period, and effective local government increasingly depends upon the achievement of a stable balance of power between the several political movements. Driven by the highly ideological atmosphere of post-Revolutionary Indonesia and the intoxication of sudden access to power, the members of the party directorates, auxiliary association governing boards, and *ad hoc* governmental committees engage in a virtually unending round of meetings, machinations, and "agit-prop" activities (demonstrations, celebrations, organizational drives, election campaigns), in an attempt to sink the still tender roots of their authority more deeply into local society.

But the traditional forms of social organization, though weakened, have far from disappeared, and consequently the *alirans* have had to make their appeal in terms of these older allegiances. The Nationalist Party finds its main roots in the civil servant class, and in those of the general population who continue to regard these white-collar administrators, technicians, accountants, and clerks as the natural leaders of society. The Communists, as one would expect, draw mainly on the landless proletariat, the former plantation workers, and the poorer peasants — the "little people" — with much of their leadership coming from the new class of young elementary and secondary school teachers created by the rapid expansion of education since the war. The *Masjumi* is led in Modjokuto by the Reform-Islam-influenced members of the merchant class and is strongest among urban businessmen; *Nahdatul Ulama* is led by the more orthodox, anti-reform Islamic elements, many of them rural Koranic teachers and scholars, and so finds most of its support in the countryside. The Communists, beginning in 1955 with the backing of about a quarter of the urban population by 1958 had gained a clear majority of the town vote, although *Nahdatul Ulama*, with its huge rural following, was the largest party in the Modjokuto region as a whole. *Masjumi* was third in size in both the town and the countryside, and the Nationalist Party, reflecting the comparative weakness of the gentry in this area, fourth. But the relationship between the parties was in no way fixed and unchangeable. The achievement of political stability within a parliamentary framework in a country neither wholly traditional nor wholly modern has proved to be as difficult on the local level in Modjokuto as it has on the national level in Djakarta.

This provisional, in-between, "no man's land" quality of Modjokuto social life is, in fact, its most outstanding characteristic. From a town composed of self-contained subcultural status groups with only minimal contact with one another, Modjokuto, under the impact of modern economic and political forces, has come more and more to consist of a mélange of mass organizations engaged in vigorous competitive interaction. Yet not only have the more traditional social loyalties not wholly dissolved and the more modern ones not wholly crystallized, but the general economic structure of the town also remains peculiarly poised between the past and the future. The plantations permanently removed Modjokuto and the countryside around it from the realm of a self-subsistent peasant economy. Today there is hardly a villager anywhere in the district who does not operate primarily in terms of the market.[5] And yet, despite thoroughgoing monetization, ex-

[5] See R. Jay, *Village Life in Modjokuto* (in press) for a detailed description of economic process in Modjokuto villages.

tensive integration into a non-local economy, and expanded and diversified effective demand, the few outstanding efforts by members of the old merchant class to create more efficient productive and distributive institutions in the town are nearly swamped by the hundreds of small-scale petty traders trying to squeeze a marginal living out of traditional commerce. The reconstruction of Modjokuto's economic life, like the reconstruction of her social structure generally, is so far but half-begun; it remains tentative, ill-defined, seemingly unable to complete itself. Bustling, fluid, "forward-looking," and yet for all that basically undynamic, the town seems stranded, at least for the moment, between the heritage of yesterday and the possibilities of tomorrow.

Tabanan: A Balinese Court Town

Almost all Bali slopes. In the center of the turtle-shaped island, rather toward its northern edge, a cluster of volcanoes rises up to heights of from five to ten thousand feet, and from the volcanoes to the seacoast some twenty to twenty-five miles to the south run a series of gradually descending spurs, cut longitudinally by deep, sheer-faced, swiftly rushing watercourses spaced five hundred to a thousand yards apart. About three-fourths of the way down along one of these spurs, in the southwestern quarter of the island, lies Tabanan, population 12,000 (826 Chinese). In precolonial times the seat of one of Bali's most powerful and cultured courts, it is today, with its row of Chinese stores, its market place, and its government offices, schools, and hospital, as typical of small-town Bali as Modjokuto is of small-town Java.

According to tradition as it appears in the palm-leaf *lontar* manuscripts of classical Bali, the Tabanan royal line, and so presumably the town of Tabanan with it, was founded about 1350 by Batara Hario Damar, one of the great, semimythical field generals of the fourteenth-century East Javanese kingdom of Madjapahit, which, it is said, brought the whole of Bali under its sway at that time. In 1906, eighteen generations of (theoretically) unbroken succession later, the ruling king of Tabanan, Nerario Ngurah Rai Perang, tricked into captivity by the Dutch who had sacked and burned his palace and were preparing to exile him, cut his throat, and the five-hundred-year dynasty was interrupted. After a twenty-year interim period, during which Tabanan was governed by the head of a junior noble line under the general surveillance of the lone Dutch official resident in the town, the closest living relative of the dead king was brought back from exile in Lombok and set upon a cardboard throne as a Dutch gesture toward "self-government." In the Japanese period this man's son, a diffident and somewhat ineffectual individual, succeeded him; but in 1955, tired by the machinations of post-revolutionary political life and feeling himself a victim of institutionalized *lèse majesté*, he abdicated. As a result, Tabanan is today the only regency in south Bali formally without a king, being ruled by a board of government officials and party leaders appointed by the island's Resident.[6] But the role of the nobility remains central. Here it has not been the bazaar but the palace which has stamped its character upon the town, not the Islamized trader but the Hinduized aristocrat who has been its distinctive figure.[7]

This fact is apparent from the very design of the town: the block-long, high-walled noble "houses" clustered on a small hill at its center around the open square where the palace of the king once stood; the small, enclosed courtyard homes of the commoners, packed solidly together in neighborhood-sized blocks down at the foot of the hill, where the general decline to the sea begins to become more regular and smooth; the market, the string of Chinese stores, the two movie theaters, and the bus depot which together form the small business section, jammed in between these upper and lower levels like a thin intruding wedge. Since the Revolution, a few bungalow-housed government offices have been

---

[6] Elsewhere in South Bali, the legitimate local king still heads the local regency (called Swapradja in Bali) administration in a compromise between traditional and modern systems of government. Elections for local political offices and regency councils have not yet been held in Bali, though they have in Java.

[7] One index of this is that about 32 per cent of the population of Tabanan is titled *vs.* a Bali-wide average of about 8 to 10 per cent (V. E. Korn, *Adatrecht van Bali* [2d rev. ed.; s'Gravenhage: no publisher, 1936]). Both these figures include not simply members of the ruling families, however, but of all members of the three upper castes: Vesia, Ksatria, and Brahmana.

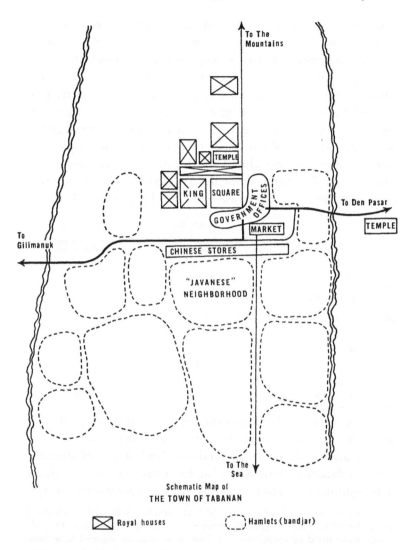

Schematic Map of
THE TOWN OF TABANAN

⊠ Royal houses ⟨˙˙˙⟩ Hamlets (bandjar)

built up on the hill, some new, rather imposing Balinese-run
stores have appeared at its foot, and the market has been enlarged;
but the sharp division between the high-born on high ground and
the low on low ground still remains. Typified by the various
pagoda-like temples scattered around the town and by the elaborate ritual processions one can see clanging their way through

the narrow streets almost any day of the week, the general effect is one of a society in which the solvent powers of a market economy and of nationalist politics are only just beginning to be felt.

This "just beginning" quality of Tabanan comes out even more strongly when the town and the countryside around it are seen against the comparative background of Modjokuto. On the urban side, the occupational structures of the two towns contrast rather strikingly: in Modjokuto about 86 per cent of the population is engaged in non-agricultural — in broad terms, "commercial" — activities, in Tabanan only about 50 per cent; in Modjokuto very few still make a living from the land, in Tabanan almost half do: [8]

	MODJOKUTO (N = 5,010) Per cent of Employed Labor Force	TABANAN (N = 2,521) Per cent of Employed Labor Force
Farmer	6	42
Storekeeper, Trader, Peddler..........	41	21
Skilled Worker, Craftsman	12	9
Unskilled Worker	34	20
Civil Servant, Teacher, Clerk..........	7	8

In the countryside, whose uneven topography covered with thousands of small, irregularly shaped, stairlike rice terraces contrasts sharply with the flat checkerboard landscape of Modjokuto, the population is both somewhat less dense — 1,200 per square mile against Modjokuto's 2,200 [9] — and less market-oriented. Un-

[8] These figures, which were drawn from election registrations in both cases, are to be taken only as general estimates not precise tabulations. In both towns, those listed as having no work (mostly women) or unnoted have been ignored, so the totals represent the active, employed labor force, though many of these people are of course "underemployed." The Chinese have not been included in the tabulation for both towns; the non-Balinese Indonesians (Javanese, Sumatrans, etc.) have not been included for Tabanan. If these two groups had been included, the contrast revealed in the table between the two towns would have been even sharper.

[9] The density figures are for the subdistrict (30 square miles) in Modjokuto, and the district (13 square miles) in Tabanan. The comparable figures for the larger units of Modjokuto District (167 square miles) and Tabanan Swa-

like the Modjokuto area (and some other parts of Bali) rice is
grown twice yearly in the villages around Tabanan, and dry cash
crops, though important in a few places, are in general not nearly
so prominent. Most peasants, in contrast to the majority of their
Javanese counterparts, are able to store enough rice to meet their
needs and are for the most part not forced to buy much food on
the open market. Agricultural wage labor and renting of rice
fields for money, both very common around Modjokuto, are here
extremely rare, although land is freely bought and sold and may
be put into pawn. Handicraft remains much stronger than in
Java, where it has almost entirely disappeared, and a certain
amount of village and kin-group craft specialization still exists. In
the absence, now or in the past, of any capital-intensive agricultural activity of the sugar-mill and plantation sort, monetization,
proletarianization, and integration into a world-wide economy
have all gone rather less far, in both town and village, than they
have in the Modjokuto area.

On the political level a similar contrast appears. Though there
are two major political parties of importance in Tabanan, as
there are in Bali generally, the Nationalist (*Partai Nasional Indonesia*, PNI) and the Socialist (*Partai Sosialis Indonesia*, PSI),
they do not have around them the whole structure of auxiliary
associations that accompanies the parties in Modjokuto, nor are
they nearly so systematically organized as in the Javanese town.
While mass-based nationalist political movements appeared in
Modjokuto as early as 1915, there were no such movements of any
kind in Tabanan until well after the beginning of the Revolution, which, in turn, disrupted Balinese society only slightly compared to the almost total upheaval it brought about in most parts

pradja (329 square miles), where there is in both cases a certain amount of
unsettled land, are 1,500 and 700 per square mile. The total populations are
for Modjokuto District: 1920 — 150,381 and 1953—248,625; for Tabanan Swapradja: 1937 — 169,270 and 1958 — 239,181. These figures yield very similar
growth rates for the two areas, 1.7 per cent annually for Tabanan, 1.5 per
cent annually for Modjokuto, but ought not to be taken as more than
approximations. Both these calculated rates are, in fact, probably somewhat
low. For Modjokuto population figures in general see Geertz, *Social Context
. . . op. cit.*, p. 77 ff. For Tabanan, I. Gusti Gde Raka, *Monografi Pulau Bali*
(Djakarta: Djawatan Pertanian, 1955).

of central Java. As a result, though nationalist politics are often
quite vigorous in Tabanan, they are expressed mainly through
the medium of traditional local institutions rather than the specially formed labor unions, women's clubs, youth groups, religious
societies, and so on. In Bali generally, political affiliation tends to
follow traditional allegiances rather closely, so that rival kin-
groups, villages, and caste groups find themselves on opposite
sides of the political fence as a mere reflex of their position in
local social structure. As yet, the persistence of customary social
forms remains strong enough to force national political processes
to realize themselves in terms of properly Balinese concerns, and
rather than shaping local loyalties, as they are increasingly coming
to do in Java, they are able only to reflect them. Although Tabanan has political parties, it has, to date, no *alirans*.[10]

Yet, having said all this about the weakening of tradition in the
Javanese town as compared to the Balinese, it is necessary to add
that the difference is rather rapidly becoming less marked; that
although it is true that Tabanan has only just begun to lose its
characteristic balance, it has definitely begun to lose it. Although
still calm, well-ordered, and somewhat self-contained, it is not
static.

The evidences of this are everywhere. Within the last five years
Balinese-run enterprises in ice manufacturing, weaving, tire recapping, and soft-drink bottling have appeared. Two large export
concerns, also Balinese-run, plus several smaller ones now handle
most of the trade in coffee, pigs, and cattle destined for Djakarta
and Singapore, once entirely in Chinese hands. A white row of
new Balinese retail stores has appeared along the main street;
two fairly large bus lines have been formed by Balinese chauf-
feurs and mechanics; several shoe factories, stores, and repair
shops flourish; there is a large new book store to serve the expanding school population; two or three new furniture shops
have opened, and so on. On the political level, the intensity of the
conflicts which led up to the abdication of the king, the expansion
of the bureaucracy to create an education-based civil servant class

[10] See H. Geertz, "The Balinese Village," and C. Geertz, "The Javanese
Village," in G. William Skinner (ed.), *National and Local Loyalties in the
Indonesian Village: A Symposium* (New Haven: Yale University Press, 1959).

independent of the traditional nobility, and the increasingly rapid growth of the still small Communist party in the town seem to herald a deeper penetration of nationalism into the local scene. Although nearly all these changes have taken place since the Revolution, the majority of them in the last three or four years, they almost certainly promise Tabanan a future radically different from its past.

But it is to the past that one must look for the roots of these contemporary tendencies toward a fundamental transformation of social and economic structure, as well as for an understanding of the dynamics of this transformation. Most particularly, it is necessary to trace the vicissitudes of the noble caste within the local society during the course of this century; for if Modjokuto's recent history is best seen in the light of alterations in the pattern of market organization, Tabanan's is most completely understood against the background of modifications in political structure. It is, again, the changing role of the aristocrat rather than of the trader which has been crucial here.

Before 1906 there were about fifteen noble houses on the hill, all of them patrilineally related to one another and to the royal family at their head. Each of these houses had the right to call on a certain number of commoner families scattered irregularly through the villages for corvée labor and military support; and with regard to these families they also had various judicative powers in certain criminal and civil matters. Together with junior houses placed in various key villages, with similar rights but fewer subjects, they formed a loose, kin-based confederation of sovereigns; the king, with the highest rank and most subjects, was the most consequential of these sovereigns but hardly a true monarch. Political ties were thus personally, not territorially organized. In each village four or five families, not necessarily related to one another, "belonged" to one noble house; ten or fifteen to the next; seven or eight to a third; and so on. And looking downward, the human "holdings" of a single noble house were almost always scattered rather than concentrated in a few neighboring villages; there was some tendency for regional clustering, only the royal house itself usually having a few families in almost every village in the kingdom so as not to lose touch with local developments.

The houses, which contained from two or three to more than a dozen elementary families but acted as solidary corporate units under the leadership of their senior male, were usually also large landholders. But landholding was not directly integrated into the political order, as it was, for example, in Western feudalism. The land belonging to the house was worked by commoner share-croppers who kept one-half of the harvest, but, in a significant number of instances, these croppers would be the political subjects not of their own landlord house but of a different one. And as taxation was organized according to the irrigation system, with a particular house having the right to tax all land irrigated from a given watercourse, a peasant might well find himself political subject of one lord, tenant of a second, and taxed by yet a third. Although in many cases some or all of these allegiences coalesced, the system was essentially one of cross-cutting personal ties, more or less deliberately designed to balance supravillage loyalties in such a way as to minimize the formation of large-scale political factions.

Such a system breeds intrigue. The politics of classical Bali consisted of rebellious conspiracies, strategic marriages, calculated affronts, and artful blandishments woven into a delicate pattern of Machiavellian statecraft that rewarded with power only those quick enough to grasp it and bold enough to use it. Their status legitimized by a revised version of the Hindu institution of caste which held them to be direct descendants of the gods, by the huge ritual celebrations, often involving the greater part of the kingdom's population, which they conducted periodically within their palace walls, and by their patronage and cultivation of the now world-famous music and theater arts of Bali, the various lords struggled continually to expand the scope of their operations through manipulation of the enormously elaborate system of social alliances in which they were enmeshed. When the Dutch came they struck at the very heart of this system: they suppressed the personal service tie between lord and subject and replaced it with a territorial bureaucratic relationship. With this kingpin removed, the traditional state was demolished at a single blow, and the position of the aristocracy could never be quite the same again.

The first equilibrating effort the lords made after Dutch incursion was to transfer the non-military aspects of the traditional service tie to their sharecroppers, thus producing a system at least superficially resembling that of medieval Europe. The work and material contributions for the lord's rituals, the repairs for the lord's palace, the labor in the lord's coconut gardens were now performed by the lord's tenants. In such a way many of the trappings and some of the substance of the traditional status of the nobility were maintained through the short period of direct colonial rule. Since the Revolution, however, even this modified basis for upper-caste pre-eminence has come under attack. Personal services by tenants to their landlords are now forbidden in theory and in practice only performed when the relations between lord and tenant remain warm. Progressive land taxation, laws protecting tenants against displacement and high rents, and the general egalitarian sentiments engendered by nationalist ideology have made landlordism a much less attractive proposition than it was in the days before the war; and in any case holdings have been much fractionated by individuation of ownership within the houses, whose populations have, in turn, multiplied as a result of better hygiene and fewer wars. On the political side, the opening of administrative posts to talents — and to political party patronage — has tended to weaken the monopolistic hold of the aristocracy on the civil service. Trade and industry, insofar as they can be profitably pursued, become means to maintain one's threatened status, wealth, and power. It is not entirely surprising to discover that it is this group of obsolete princelings who are, in the main, behind Tabanan's recent economic expansion.

In precolonial times all foreign trade in the kingdom — the main export was coffee, the main import opium — was conducted by a single wealthy Chinese called a *subandar*, who held a royal monopoly in exchange for a suitable tribute, the remainder of the small resident Chinese population acting as his agents. Domestic trade was trifling, conducted in small, local markets and by a few itinerant textile peddlers. Such a market was held once in three days in a small square in the shadow of the wall of the royal palace in Tabanan, where a dozen or so women sold spices, coconut oil, palm wine, earthenware and other goods for a few hours in the morning. After the beginning of direct Dutch rule, the market moved down to join the few Chinese stores at the foot of the hill and began to expand both in volume and variety of goods. The leading merchants in this still restricted growth were, however, not Balinese but fifty to a hundred Indonesians from other parts of the archipelago, particularly from the coastal regions along the Java Sea in Sumatra, Java, Borneo, and the Celebes, who migrated to the town during the generally prosperous 1910–30 period. Referred to collectively as "Javanese people" (*anak Djawa*), which the majority of them were, they represented the same piously Islamic, market-born-and-bred group of adroit traders who in Modjokuto became the town's leading citizens. They lived segregated in a mosque-centered, Java-style, unwalled neighborhood behind the Chinese stores, became the butchers, furniture-makers, tailors, shoemakers, restaurant-keepers, cloth merchants, tobacco-traders, and vegetable-sellers of Tabanan's first serious involvement in the all-Indonesian bazaar economy, and injected their distinctive Levantine note into the town's generally Hinduist ethos. But, lacking the stimulus of Modjokuto's plantation economy and being "foreigners" both religiously and ethnically (they regarded the Balinese as pork-eating infidels; the Balinese thought of them as uncultured cheats), they could achieve nothing approaching the central role they played in Modjokuto. Their activities remained limited and non-fermentative, easily contained within the boundaries of an intrusive and culturally insulated business community. Only with the entry of Balinese upper-caste entrepreneurs into the realm of commerce since the war has trade begun to exercise a dynamic effect on Tabanan social life generally.

Thus the fundamental instability introduced into Tabanan's complex, volatile, but nevertheless delicately balanced social system by the Dutch displacement of the indigenous aristocracy from their position at its political center begins, fifty years later, to have its effect on the economic structure of the society. The "just beginning" quality of the town's modernization is in part misleading, for the sources of the changes now occurring can be traced back to the sacking of Tabanan in 1906. The suicide of the old king (and of his son, the crown prince, who followed him into oblivion by means of an overdose of opium) represented in a quite literal sense the death of the old order; and the contemporary movement of his heirs today into the still only partly formed world of trade and industry represents the birth — whether it ultimately proves to be abortive or not — of a new one. Economic leadership, which in Modjokuto has fallen to the successors of the Islam-oriented, north coast commercial elite of the tens and twenties, has fallen in Tabanan to the succesors of the Hinduized, caste-insulated, political elite of the pre-Revolutionary state.

3. Economic Development in Modjokuto

In Modjokuto, the problem of economic development presents itself primarily as an organizational one. What the entrepreneurial group of Islamic small businessmen most lacks is not capital, for in terms of the realistic opportunities for innovation which they actually have, their resources are not inadequate; not drive, for they display the typically "Protestant" virtues of industry, frugality, independence, and determination in almost excessive abundance; certainly not a sufficient market, for the possibilities for significant expansion of both trade and industry stand apparent in Modjokuto on all sides. What they lack is the power to mobilize their capital and channel their drive in such a way as to exploit the existing market possibilities. They lack the capacity to form efficient economic institutions; they are entrepreneurs without enterprises.

As noted above, Modjokuto from its beginning has had a bazaar economy, i.e., one in which the total flow of commerce is fragmented into a very great number of unrelated person-to-person transactions. In contrast to the firm-centered economy of the West, where trade and industry occur through a set of impersonally defined social institutions which organize a variety of specialized occupations with respect to some particular productive or distributive end, this sort of economy is based on the independent activities of a set of highly competitive commodity traders who relate to one another mainly by means of an incredible volume of *ad hoc* acts of exchange. Although such an economy has the advantage that it can employ vast numbers of people on a marginal or near-marginal level of living, it has the disadvantage that it turns even the established businessman away from an interest in reducing costs and developing markets and toward petty speculation and short-run opportunism. In the absence of developed organizational forms in terms of which to make sustained collective economic activity possible, the bazaar-trader is unable actively to search out and create new sources of profit; he can only grasp occasions for gain as they fitfully and, from his point of view, spontaneously arise.

Progress toward more effective patterns of economic activity in Modjokuto consequently takes the form of a movement, hesitant and circumscribed, away from a bazaar-type economy toward a firm-type economy. It is the creation, or attempted creation, of firm or firm-like distributive or productive institutions, of small stores, service shops and factories, which represents the process of development in the present state of Modjokuto's economy. Out of the diffuse, individualistic, confused tumult of the market place, a few of the more ambitious members of the town's established trading class are attempting, as did their fathers before them, to organize their activities in a more systematic manner and conduct them on a larger scale. Without the stimulus of an expanding, locally based export trade, even of an enclave sort, and hampered by the tremendous overcrowding of the market network by marginal operators, these men face an even more difficult task than did their fathers. But they have the advantages of political freedom and, particularly if significant expansion of trade and industry takes place in the country as a whole, they may yet enjoy a happier fate than befell the victims of the great depression. In any case, in the means they use and the obstacles they face in their endeavor to move out of the world of the market place and into the world of the business establishment, they display most clearly the characteristic texture of the problem of economic growth as it appears in Modjokuto today.

The Bazaar Type Economy: The Traditional Pasar[1]

The *pasar* (probably from the Persian "bāzār" by the way of
Arabic), or traditional market, is at once an economic institution
and a way of life, a general mode of commercial activity reaching
into all aspects of Modjokuto society, and a sociocultural world
nearly complete in itself. As agriculture for the peasant, so petty
commerce provides for the trader the permanent backdrop against
which almost all his activities occur. It is his environment — as
much, from his perspective, a natural phenomenon as a cultural
one — and the whole of his life is shaped by it. Thus by the *pasar*
we mean not simply that particular square eighth of a mile or so
of sheds and platforms, set apart in the center of the town, where
(as someone has said of the classical emporium) men are permitted each day to deceive one another, but the whole pattern
of small-scale peddling and processing activity characteristic of
the Modjokuto area generally. The market place is the climax of
this pattern, its focus and center, but it is not the whole of it;
for the *pasar* style of trading permeates the whole region, thin-
ning out somewhat only in the most rural of the villages.

To understand the *pasar* in this broad sense, one needs to look
at it from three points of view: first, as a patterned flow of economic goods and services; second, as a set of economic mechanisms
to sustain and regulate that flow of goods and services, and third
as a social and cultural system in which those mechanisms are
imbedded.

THE FLOW OF GOODS AND SERVICES

From the point of view of the flow of goods and services, the most
salient characteristic of the *pasar* is the sort of material with
which it mainly deals: unbulky, easily portable, easily storable
foodstuffs, textiles, small hardware and the like, whose inventories can be increased or decreased gradually and by degrees;
goods which permit marginal alterations in the scale of trading
operations rather than demanding discontinuous "jumps." In

[1] For a general empirical description of the Modjokuto market see A.
Dewey, *Peasant Marketing in Java* (New York: Free Press, 1962).

cases where a discontinuous jump is involved between small- and large-scale operations (furniture is an example), the *pasar* traders always remain small. It is only in those goods whose investment curve is continuous along its entire length (for example, textiles) where you sometimes find rather large-scale market-type traders. For the others — dry season crops, household furnishings, prepared foods, etc. — market traders tend to control the trade up to the point where marginal increases in inventory can no longer be profitably made. On the other side of the "jump" from peddling to merchandising, the Chinese storekeepers, truckers, and warehouse owners have — with a few striking exceptions — complete control.

In any case, whatever the wares, turnover is very high, and volume in any one sale very small. Goods flow through the market channels at a dizzying rate, not as broad torrents but as hundreds of little trickles, funneled through an enormous number of transactions. And this flow of goods is anything but direct: the proportion of retail sales (in the sense of sale to a consumer) to wholesale sales (in the sense of sale to another seller) within the *pasar* is rather small. Commodities, at least non-perishable ones, once injected into the market network tend to move in circles, passing from trader to trader for a fairly extended period before they come within the reach of a genuine consumer. One piece of cloth often has ten or a dozen owners between the time it leaves the Chinese-owned factory in a nearby city and the time it is finally sold to someone in a Modjokuto village who seems likely to use it. A basket of maize may be sold by a peasant to a local village trader, who carries it to market and sells it to a second trader, who in turn sells it to a larger market-trader, who gathers it together with similar baskets from other petty traders and sells it to a local Chinese, who ships it to Surabaja to another Chinese, after which it may begin the whole process in reverse in some other area.[2] Like Javanese agriculture, Javanese trading is highly labor intensive; and perhaps the best, if slightly caricatured image for it is that of a long line of men passing bricks from hand to hand over some greatly extended distance to build, slowly and brick by brick, a large wall.

[2] See *Ibid.* for detailed descriptions of such processes.

The other aspect of the flow of goods and services which needs to be emphasized is that most of the processing and manufacturing activities which take place in Modjokuto are also included within it. Simple processing (mostly drying) of crops is perhaps the most elementary example. But bamboo-weaving, garment-making, food-preparing (there are hundreds of small restaurants and coffee shops), house-building, and various sorts of repair work — bicycle, shoe, watch, blacksmith, etc. — are also integrated into the general system. So are the more purely service trades, such as haircutting, and horse-cart or pedi-cab transport. The *pasar* must not be seen simply as a distributive apparatus which adds no real value to the goods which flow through it. It is a manufacturing, productive apparatus as well, and the two elements, the movement of goods and their processing — insofar as this is accomplished in Modjokuto — are wholly intertwined. Production, distribution, and sales are fused into one comprehensive economic institution.[3]

REGULATORY MECHANISMS

As for the set of economic mechanisms which sustain and regulate this flow of goods and services, three are of central importance: (1) a sliding price system, (2) a complex balance of carefully managed credit relationships, (3) an extensive fractionation of risks and, as a corollary, of profit margins.

The sliding price system, accompanied by the colorful and often aggressive bargaining which seems to mark such systems everywhere, is in part simply a means of communicating economic information in an indeterminate pricing situation. The continual haggling over terms is to a degree a mere reflex of the fact that the absence of complex bookkeeping and long-run cost or budget-

---

[3] Of course, the processing value added locally to the goods which flow through the market is a very small percentage of such value as a whole. Most of the manufactured goods sold in the market are produced outside the Modjokuto area, often outside Indonesia. The argument here is simply that, with the partial exception of the more differentiated manufacturing enterprises we shall discuss below, what processing and manufacturing activities do take place in the local area are structurally part and parcel of the *pasar* pattern.

ary accounting makes it difficult for either the buyer or the seller to calculate very exactly what, in any particular case, a "reasonable" price is. Pricing is much more a matter of estimates in a situation where highly specific comparative and historical data are simply not available; instead of exactly calculated prices, one finds the setting of broad limits within which buyer and seller explore together the finer details of the matter through a system of offer and counteroffer. The ability to operate effectively in the gap of ignorance between a price obviously too high and one obviously too low is what makes a good market-trader: skill in bargaining — which includes as its elements a quick wit, a tireless persistence, and an instinctive shrewdness in evaluating men and material on the basis of very little evidence — is his primary professional qualification.

Even more important, however, the sliding price system tends to create a situation in which the primary competitive stress is not between seller and seller, as it is for the most part in a firm economy, but between buyer and seller.[4] The fixed price system, along with brand names, advertising, and the other economic customs which accompany it, relieves the buyer-seller relation of competitive pressure and places it on the relations between sellers. Lacking fixed prices, *pasar* competition takes a rather different form from that to which, except to a degree in the automobile and real-estate markets, we are accustomed: the buyer pits his knowledge of the contemporary state of the market, as well as his stubbornness and persistence, against a similar knowledge on the part of a seller, as well as the latter's nerve and *his* stubbornness. The characteristics of a "good" buyer and a "good" seller are thus identical. In fact, there is little if any differentiation between the buying role and the selling role as long as one remains within the *pasar*; the trader is either or both indifferently. The relatively high percentage of wholesale transactions (i.e., transactions in which goods are bought with the express intention to resell them) means that in most cases both buyer and seller are professional traders and the contest is one between experts.

[4] See T. Parsons and N. Smelzer, *Economy and Society* (Glencoe, Ill.: Free Press, 1956).

When the sale is "retail" and the buyer is not a professional trader, then the seller clearly has a marked advantage, and Javanese commercial folklore is replete with stories of sharp traders deceiving gullible peasants.

In fact, the general reputation of the bazaar-type trader for "unscrupulousness," "lack of ethics," etc., arises mainly from this role asymmetry in the retail market in a bazaar economy, rather than from an uninhibited, normatively unregulated expression of the "acquisitive impulse" as Max Weber and others seem to think.[5] Within the *pasar* context "let the buyer beware" is a challenge rather than a ruthless or amoral attitude, a reasonable and legitimate expectation for a seller to have, and is accepted as such by a buyer; in any case, it is balanced by an equally strong "let the seller beware." If everyone in the society were a trader, there would be little problem. It is when the villager, manual laborer, or civil servant comes up against this sort of pure and unmixed trader, and the warning "let the seller beware" is unheeded due to the buyer's lack of commercial skills, that the complaints begin to arise, as witness the nearly world-wide fear, hatred, and suspicion which peasants have for traders.

This tendency for competition to be stressed between buyer and seller rather than between sellers has yet other effects on the general style of commercial life. In a fully developed firm economy,

[5] "The *auri sacri fames* of a Neapolitan cabdriver . . . and certainly of Asiatic representatives of similar trades as well as of the craftsmen of southern Europe or Asiatic countries, is, as anyone can find out for himself, very much more intense, and especially more unscrupulous than that of, say an Englishman in similar circumstances. The universal reign of absolute unscrupulousness in the pursuit of selfish interests by the making of money has been a specific characteristic of precisely those countries whose bourgeois-capitalistic development, measured according to Occidental standards, has remained backward." M. Weber, *The Protestant Ethic and the Spirit of Capitalism*, trans. T. Parsons (New York and London: Scribner, 1930), pp. 56–57. Similarly, Weber's view was that market relationships in traditional China stood, in Parsons' paraphrase "outside [the category of moral valuation] in a realm of ethical indifference, with a general unwillingness to assume ethical obligations," T. Parsons, *The Structure of Social Action* (Glencoe, Ill.: Free Press, 1949), p. 551. This view, curious for a scholar who elsewhere consistently insisted on the central role of norms in structuring social behavior, seems to derive from an assumption that because the ethical code of the trading classes is not that of the wider society in which they are imbedded, they lack a code altogether.

price, less subject to bargaining pressure from the individual buyer, is, so far as any single transaction is concerned, generally not problematical. What is problematical is somehow getting someone to buy at a particular price. Consequently, a merchant tends to regard his primary task as one of creating or stimulating buyers, through advertising, aggressive salesmanship, choosing a strategic location, building a reputation, providing better service, or offering "greater" value in the sense of a lower over-all price level. In the *pasar*, conditions are reversed. Traders often say quite explicitly that finding prospective customers is not a problem in their minds: they either come or they do not, the market is either crowded or it is not; and whatever the causes may be for the flurries and dead spots which so mark *pasar* trading, they are not within the control of the trader. True, people will choose a normally busy market over a normally dull one. One naturally goes where the buyers and sellers are likely to be and where deals are being made. But the idea is not so much to create or stimulate a market for whatever you have to sell; rather it is to be present when a chance to sell appears, and most especially, to be capable of making the most of it. If you ask Modjokuto traders whether they feel envious if a customer goes to the booth next to them (all the people selling a given ware are lined up next to one another in one section of the market place) they say no, that it is wholly a matter of chance, and if the customer does not buy from a neighbor he will in all probability come to them next, or another customer will come along in a few minutes. But they do feel depressed when a customer who has come to them does not buy (especially after a protracted bargaining session with him), for that is their failure; they have had their chance and have failed to capitalize on it.

The bargaining, sliding price pattern thus tends to focus all the trader's attention on the individual two-person transaction: the aim is always to get as much as possible out of the deal immediately at hand. The *pasar* trader is perpetually looking for a chance to make a smaller or larger killing, not attempting to build up a stable clientele or a steadily growing business. He sees his activities as a set of essentially unrelated exchanges with a very

wide variety of trading partners and customers, which taken together form no over-all pattern and build toward no cumulative
end. Similarly, traders tend to think of the average business career
not as a Horatio Alger rags-to-riches pattern of linear progress, but
as a series of cycles in which one oscillates, more or less rapidly,
between being ahead of the game and being behind it, between
being well off and being bankrupt. The sliding price provides
the flexibility needed in a system where economic conditions
are unstable, market information poor, and trading hyperindividuated; but it does so at the cost of stimulating an essentially
speculative, *carpe diem* attitude toward commerce.

The second economic mechanism of importance in the *pasar*
context is a complex and ramified network of credit balances bind-
ing larger and smaller traders together. It is this network which
provides the primary integrative factor in the *pasar*, for it leads
to a hierarchic ranking of traders in which larger traders give
credit to smaller ones and smaller ones have debts to larger ones.
These credit balances are only half-understood if they are seen
only as ways in which capital is made available, for they set
up and stabilize more or less persisting commercial relationships.
If this element is taken into account, the seemingly anomalous
fact that traders often prefer expensive private credit to cheap
government credit becomes clearer. Private credit gives them more
than simple access to capital; it secures their position in the flow
of trade.

The way in which this pattern works has been well-described
by T'ien in his study of the rubber trade among the Sarawak
Chinese: [6]

Debt accumulation works as follows: a small outstanding
sum of say, about $20 starts the ball rolling; once the small
rural shop owner can get even this much credit he is well on
the way to forcing his creditor to give him almost unlimited
credit in the future, under the generally accepted recognition
that the full debt never will be paid off unless further credit
is forthcoming. For instance, on opening a new relationship

[6] Ju-Kang T'ien, *The Chinese of Sarawak*, Monographs on Social Anthropology No. 12 (London: London School of Economics and Political Science,
n.d.), p. 95.

with a shop of the second rank a rural shop-owner will be very careful to pay the first two or three accounts promptly and in full. In this way he establishes his reputation, and then, later, he may ask for, say 5% or 10% allowance on his next account, giving the excuse that he just happens to be short of money for the time being. Of course the bazaar shopkeeper understands what is happening, but he has his own interest to consider as well, and he knows that unless he grants credit in this way he will be able to do no business at all – and in any case, he has probably acquired almost all his own stock of goods from Singapore in a similar way. Once the debt has been started in this courteous manner, the debtor will probably try to increase the amount advanced to him each time – say to 20% or 30% or the total account. The more unscrupulous debtors may go so far as to demand a full 100%. The creditor knows that if he refuses he will lose the debt already outstanding, for his customer will transfer his business elsewhere. Payment or part payment of an outstanding debt is thus by convention the accepted method of acquiring fresh credit.

T'ien emphasizes here the hold the debtor has over the creditor, but the reverse is true as well: the creditor has a hold over the debtor in that he provides him with the basis of doing business at all. Actually, the larger the debt grows, *assuming a more or less constant volume of transactions between the two traders*, the stronger the position of the debtor; the smaller it stays, the stronger the position of the creditor, recalling Keynes's comment that if you owe your banker a thousand dollars you are in his power, but if you owe him a million he is in yours. Thus in any credit relationship the creditor will attempt to keep the credit balance as small as possible, i.e., keep things on as much of a cash basis as he can; while the debtor will try to keep the credit balance as large as possible, i.e., keep things on as much of a credit basis as possible. We have here but another version of the bargaining relationship. The problem is to keep the credit balance neither too large nor too small relative to any given level of trading activity between two partners. If it gets too large, the temptation for the debtor to default (legal enforcement of *pasar* debts is virtually impossible) becomes very strong, tending to override the damage to reputation involved in such behavior. If it gets too small, the debtor will simply try some other, more yielding creditor, and the relationship will come to an end. The balance must be large enough to keep the trade relation between the larger and smaller trader healthy and active, and small enough not to lead to default and an irrecoverable loss for the creditor.

How large is "large enough, but not too large" is of course dependent upon a variety of factors: the reputation of the debtor for reliability as well as his skill as a trader; the non-economic ties between creditor and debtor which either can use as sanctions; the comparative economic strength of the two parties, etc. The most general pattern in Modjokuto, however, is for a creditor to give a debtor a certain, not-too-great amount of goods wholly on credit to initiate the relationship. After the latter has sold these goods, he will pay back half the debt. For example, if he receives Rp. 30 worth of cloth, he will pay back Rp. 15, leaving a Rp. 15 debt. He then may take Rp. 30 more cloth, paying half in cash, thus raising his total debt to Rp. 30 again. How much of this debt he will pay off after selling the cloth this time depends upon how the relationship is developing, but between Rp. 5 and Rp. 10 would be usual, thus reducing his debt to Rp. 20 or Rp. 25. In this way, the debt tends to revolve around Rp. 30, the first advance, being either a few rupiah less or a few more at all times. If it is more, the creditor will put pressure on the debtor to reduce it; if it is less, the debtor will put pressure on the creditor to let him have more goods on credit. If the whole relationship works out well, the creditor may permit the whole debt to rise slowly, thus increasing the volume of transactions between himself and the debtor. But in any normal credit relationship there seems usually to be a certain level of indebtedness and volume which, once reached, tends to be maintained, in which persistent expectations are set up on both sides such that both will tend to agree at any particular point in time whether the debt is too large or too small.[7]

[7] Of course in addition to the bargaining process centering around the size of the allowable debt, there is a bargaining about the price to be charged for goods and this is not unaffected by whether or how far one pays by cash. In-

There is in such a system a tendency to try always to trade with someone else's capital. Even people with enough cash at the time to buy, say, a few baskets of kapok for which they have a buyer in mind will not, if they can help it, invest their own money but will look around for credit. Yet they may at the same time advance credit, even lend cash, to others for other deals. The wry saying T'ien reports from Sarawak — "Buy for ten, sell for seven, give back three and keep four" (i.e., buy an article on credit for $10, sell it to a customer for $7, and then pay the creditor $3 and keep $4) — also characterizes the Javanese attitude toward credit: its main function is not simply to capitalize trade but to stabilize and regularize ties between traders, to give persistence and form to commercial relationships. From the financial point of view, the *pasar* consist of a complex of debts carefully managed, largely in bargaining terms, to keep trade active and yet not disrupt it. Much of everyone's time is consumed in pursuing debtors and dunning them, or in trying to wheedle a little more credit from one's creditors. Such a market can be seen as a sort of hydraulic system in which the resolution of credit-balance pressures at hundreds of larger and smaller couplings determines speed, direction, and volume of the flow of goods through the system.

The role of cash in such a system is primarily one of lubricating the couplings. Cash enables one to get credit, and it is seen mainly in that light; its major uses are as a "down payment" to start the flow of credit and as "payment on account" to keep it running. The better and larger traders, at least, have a reputation for extreme thrift and asceticism; they approve as little of spending money for consumption as do the most dour of Scots Calvinists. But they do not accumulate liquid reserves in order to hire labor, land, capital equipment for more highly systematized productive purposes but to enable themselves to cut in on a large number of profitable deals. Maximizing trade volume and turnover is the aim, and cash in hand is an essential tool in the realization of such an aim. The result is an extreme and chronic hunger for cash, a very high rate of interest as a price for borrowing such cash, an

terest as an empirically isolable phenomenon appears only in the lending of cash; in credit relations it is concealed in the sliding price system.

almost complete absence of idle liquid funds, a tremendous velocity of circulation for money, and a strong aversion to establishing
high levels of equity in the objects with which they trade. Cash
is the means by which the credit system is controlled, it is the most
flexible form of economic power and is, in consequence, very
highly valued indeed. The passion for liquidity remains continually at a fever pitch in a bazaar economy.

Finally, despite the aim to maximize one's trading activities,
to increase the percentage of total traffic that passes through one's
own hands, there is also a tendency to spread oneself thin over
a very wide range of deals rather than to plunge deeply on any
one. Putting all one's eggs in a single basket is not a favored
mode of procedure; though *pasar* traders have a basically speculative orientation they strongly prefer a complicated process of
hedging to playing long shots. (The legends of great coups and
great disasters common in some of our own more fluid markets —
e.g., the grain and real-estate markets — are conspicuous by their
absence; the gambler is not a culture hero.) As a result, large,
or even moderately large, single deals with only two people involved are very rare, even in cases where the traders are large
enough to handle such deals alone. Both large and small transactions usually involve a multiplicity of people, each making a small
contribution and each taking out a small return. A trader contracting even a fairly petty agreement will look for others to go
in with him; and, in fact, there is widely felt normative obligation
on the part of traders to allow other people to cut into a good
thing. The individualism of the *pasar* traders refers to the fact
that they operate independently of any persisting economic organization, make decisions entirely in terms of their own interests
as they conceive them, and relate to each other wholly through
separate person-to-person agreements; but this does not mean that
alliances among traders are not extremely common. The individual trader, unless he is very small indeed, is the center of a
series of rapidly forming and dissolving one-deal, compositely
organized trading coalitions.

As investment is fragmented into small units and distributed
among a plurality of people, so also are profits. Risks are lessened

and returns with them. The *pasar* trader is a true marginal businessman; his world is one of a few rupiah here and a few there,
though with some individuals these bits and pieces may amount
to significant sums. And when transactions are larger than this
he divides them up so that they can be handled in such a fashion;
those which cannot be so divided almost inevitably fall to the
Chinese. Of course, in part this is simply a matter of lack of capital
resources. But it is not entirely so, for with the same capital resources a truly collective rather than simply composite organization could occur and would be more effective. For example,
suppose a peasant A offers a hundred rupiahs' worth of onions
to a *pasar* trader, B; B will urge C, D, and E to take part of the
deal, each man contracting separately with the peasant:

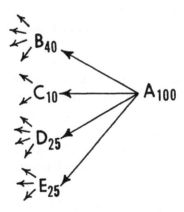

Each then will sell the crop to other buyers as occasions arise.
But with the same capital the deal could have been organized as
a genuinely collective one in which B, C, D, and E pool capital to
form a "corporation" and buy the crop as a unit and resell it:

$$\leftarrow B, C, D, E_{100} \leftarrow A_{100}$$

Not only is such genuinely corporate activity uncommon — and
on more than a one-deal basis almost nonexistent — but in many
cases B alone (or with C only) has the resources to swing the deal,
but prefers to enter one or more additional coalitions for another
commodity with F, G, and H, vis-à-vis peasant I, rather than con-
centrating his efforts.

Thus, the tendency to spread risks and profits, even on very small deals, is in large part a habitual reaction of *pasar* traders, a characteristic mode of pursuing commerce, based on a particular sort of trading outlook, which would persist for a long time even if capital were to become much more easily available. Of course, such diversification of interests and consequent spreading of risks is, like the other mechanisms described here, far from unknown or unimportant in more developed economies. It is merely the lengths to which it is carried which is here distinctive.

SOCIAL AND CULTURAL CHARACTERISTICS

Finally, as a social and cultural system the *pasar* is characterized by a traditionally "interstitial" position within Javanese society generally; by a highly developed division of labor which, in the absence of firms, guilds, well-established commercial associations, etc., provides directly the major basis of social-structural organization for the market as a whole, and by a very sharp segregation of specifically economic from diffusely non-economic social ties.

From a historical point of view, the main reason for the interstitial position of the *pasar* within Javanese society is that it is, for the most part, not a local growth but was introduced from outside at a point when Java had already achieved very high levels of social, political, and religious development. "Strange though it may seem," Henri Pirenne has written of Europe,[8]

. . . medieval commerce developed from the beginning under the influence not of local but of export trade. It was this alone which gave birth to that class of professional merchants which was the chief instrument of the economic revival of the 11th and 12th centuriees. In both parts of Europe where in started, Northern Italy and the Low Countries, the story is the same. The impetus was given by long distance trade.

For Java, the case is, in its broadest outlines, similar. The driving force in urban economic development has consistently been neither local trade nor local manufacture, though both of these have existed as far back as we can trace, but long-distance, ulti-

---

[8] H. Pirenne, *Economic and Social History of Medieval Europe* (Harvest Edition; New York: Harcourt, Brace, 1956), pp. 140–41.

mately international, trade. Long-distance trade both united the
various regions of Java into a single commercial network and connected the island as a whole to the vital trade lines of the world-
wide commercial economy. And it was only in the fourteenth
century and the centuries immediately following it, at the point
where Madjapahit, Java's glorious kingdom, crowned more than
a thousand years of political and cultural evolution under the
aegis of Hinduism, that this single network was forged and the
pasar pattern took its characteristic historical form.[9]

The relatively sudden quantitative expansion of the flow of
South Asian trade which took place from the end of the fourteenth
century onward created a whole new pattern of life along the
Javanese north coast. The integral kingdom of Madjapahit dis-
integrated, replaced by a whole series of small, trade-centered
harbor states along both sides of the Java Sea; Islam replaced
Hinduism as the dominant creed; and a fluid, egalitarian, out-
ward-looking society arose to challenge the hierarchic isolationism
of the agrarian interior. And, particularly after European dominance of interisland trade began to be effective, this new pattern
of life came to insinuate itself throughout the island as a whole.
Itinerant traders traveling along fairly well-defined market cir-
cuits provided a link between local and international economies.
A culturally homogeneous group, they formed a well-defined,
sharply set-apart minority — *wong dagang*, the Javanese word for

[9] This view is not in contradiction to that of Van Leur (J. C. Van Leur,
Indonesian Trade and Society: Essays in Asian Social and Economic History
[The Hague and Bandung, 1955]) to the effect that as a general type international trade is a "historical constant" in Indonesia, tracing back to earlier
times, or to the view that significant local and regional markets existed in
interior Java well prior to the fourteenth century. But I do hold that the
trade expansion coincident with Islamization and the rise of the north coast
kingdoms was great enough quantitatively to have had crucial qualitative
effects on Javanese social structure and culture, and that the arguments of
Van Leur. and to a lesser extent, Schrieke (B. Schrieke, *Indonesian Sociological Studies*, I [New York: Institute of Pacific Relations, 1955]) that it introduced "nothing new" into Indonesian society are inaccurate. For a discussion
of the nest of problems in historical interpretation involved here, see my
"The Development of the Javanese Economy: A Socio-Cultural Approach,"
(Boston: Massachusetts Institute of Technology, 1956); and J. Van der Kroef,
"On the Writing of Indonesian History," *Pacific Affairs*, XXXI, No. 4 (1958)
352–71.

trader, still also means "foreigner" as well as "wanderer" or "tramp" — whose values deviated in major respects from those embraced by both the gentry and the peasantry. We have seen how the representatives of this peripatetic merchant class who came to Modjokuto formed their own neighborhood, followed their own style of living, and pursued their particular businesses in general social and cultural independence of the larger community. And, even today, when the market network has been crowded by refugees from the villages and the urban working classes, this quality of intrusiveness, of incongruity and alienness, still clings to the bazaar-trader.

The main result of this social segregation has been that the *pasar* has tended to form a fairly self-contained cultural universe for its participants, while at the same time the status of the trader in the wider society has been ambiguous at best, pariah-like at worst. One cannot fully understand the bazaar-trader, and so the bazaar economy in general, unless one realizes that trading in and of itself, trading for trading's sake is one of the primary goals of his life. The trader sees trade as a peasant sees agriculture, or as a civil servant sees administration — as the expression of his essential self. As the peasant takes pride in his farming abilities and the civil servant in his executive talents, so the trader takes pride in his trading skills. Yet though both the peasant's plodding industriousness and the civil servant's subtle adeptness have had a secure pleace in the traditional Javanese value hierarchy, the trader's hardheaded shrewdness has had a much less secure one and the tendency on the part of the average man to despise the technics of commerce has always been very strong. In this sense, the Javanese too have tended to see the trader as standing "outside" the ethical order, even though the processes of trade are hedged around with very definite and explicit concepts of right and wrong, and the sanctions for enforcing these concepts are far from undeveloped or ineffectual. This historically persistent tension between the value system of the general society and that of the interstitial bazaar culture, and between peasant and gentleman on the one hand and trader on the other, is of obvious importance in the analysis of Modjokuto's development.

Perhaps the most notable single characteristic of the *pasar* pattern, especially when it is compared to similar bazaar economies in China or medieval Europe, is the absence of any sort of guild organization. Among neither traders nor craftsmen are there any persistent corporate groups with any sort of regulative powers over their members; nor, with the partial exception of the prewar trade associations which were in any case not true guilds, do there seem ever to have been any. The major structural pattern for the whole market is consequently given directly by the division of labor, the "occupational system" itself.

This division of labor takes place along two major axes: according to one's place in the over-all distributive network; or according to the sort of goods one sells. Certain traders are wholly concerned with carrying goods by bicycle between local market places, with traveling to the villages to sell, with weighing produce, or with wholesaling to other traders; others are mainly defined by the fact that they sell textiles, baskets, livestock, or maize.[10] For most traders their particular occupational role is defined along both these axes, and there is a relatively high stability in such terms. In what is otherwise a very fluid system, the tendency for most individuals to persist in one sort of trading rather than shifting easily among various sorts is of course evidence of the full-time, technically demanding, non-amateur nature of the trader role as an occupation.

In fact, the trader role seems to be almost hyperspecialized into subtypes, the *pasar* occupational structure overdifferentiated, somewhat like those featherbedded American trade unions in which one man may sweep the floor but another "specialist" must hold the dust pan. The specializations in the *pasar* case are not in any way rigidly enforced, but they are quite real: a listing of the different market roles phenomenologically discriminated by Modjokuto traders would fill several pages. And the major reason for this hyperspecialization of roles is the same as in the featherbedded trade union case: an excess of personnel who need to be employed relative to the specifically economic functions that need to be fulfilled. Only here it is not that economic progress has reduced labor force requirements too rapidly for smooth organiza-

[10] For an empirical description of these roles and the manner in which they function see Dewey, *op. cit.*

tional readjustment to occur, but that in the absence of significant economic progress a rapidly rising labor force has had to be absorbed into an essentially unchanging structure. In some respects, the problems of "overdevelopment" and "underdevelopment" take a similar form.

Finally, relationships between traders (and between traders and customers) are highly specific: commercial ties are carefully insulated from general social ties. Friendship, neighborliness, even kinship are one thing, trade is another; and the impersonal, calculating, rationalistic approach to economic activity which has sometimes been held to characterize only advanced economies is present in the Modjokuto *pasar* to a marked degree. The market is the one institutional structure in Javanese society where the formalism, status consciousness, and introversion so characteristic of the culture generally are relatively weak: bargaining, credit balances, and trade coalitions all respond quite directly and explicitly to the narrow concerns of material advantage. Whatever "traditionalism" may mean — and the *pasar* pattern dates back at least to the fourteenth century — commerce in Modjokuto is largely free of the constraints of diffusely defined cultural norms. In general, business is business.

In fact, all four of the quartet of defining attributes — specificity, universalism, achievement, and neutrality — commonly held to be distinctive of highly developed economic structures are characteristic of the *pasar* pattern as well.[11] Traders not only treat each other in precisely formulated and technically restricted terms — so that the diffuse social categories of age, sex, rank, and so on enter but slightly into the definition of the relationship — but they do so largely independently of particularistic ties. A man and his brother, a son and his father, even a wife and her husband will commonly operate on their own at the bazaar and regard one another within that context with nearly as cold an eye as they

[11] For the relation of these "pattern variables" to economic processes generally see Parsons and Smelzer, *op. cit.*; for their application to the analysis of development see M. Levy, Jr., "Contrasting Factors in the Modernization of China and Japan," in S. Kuznets, W. E. Moore and J. Spengler (eds.), *Economic Growth: Brazil, India, Japan* (Durham, N.C.: Duke University Press, 1955).

would any other trader. A man who wishes to launch a son or nephew in trade usually will not make the boy his apprentice, but rather will provide him with some goods on credit and send him off to peddle them as best he can, expecting to maintain the normal sort of credit-balance relationship with the fledgeling. Of course, there is a fairly sharp limit to the degree to which close personal ties can be overridden by technical considerations in any economy, and particularistic relationships are often used both to enforce obligations and to gain assistance; but in general, traders are nearly unanimous in emphasizing that relatives prefer to operate independently in the *pasar* and that non-economic ties of any sort ought not to have important effects on the conduct of commerce. Further, social standing within the bazaar, which is almost wholly based on the scale of one's activities and the extent of one's wealth, is clearly largely achieved, and rapid mobility, both upward and downward, is common. And as for impersonality, money, say the traders, is money, people are people, and the two ought not to be confused.

In short, whatever is obstructing the development of a modern economy out of the general background of the bazaar economy, it is not a lack of a "business-like" orientation on the part of the *pasar* traders. Commercial activities are not here entangled in an awkward and complicated fabric of social prejudices and obligations which inhibit rational calculation, egoistic behavior, or technical proficiency. The bazaar economy is traditional in the sense that its functioning is regulated by fixed customs of trade hallowed by centuries of continuous use, but not in the sense that it represents a system in which economic behavior is not very well differentiated from other sorts of social behavior. What the bazaar economy lacks is not elbow room but organization, not freedom but form.

The Firm Type Economy: Toko and Perusahaan

The exact nature of the task of innovation facing Modjokuto's would-be entrepreneurial class is conditioned, therefore, by two main determinants: the general character of the *pasar* as an economic institution, and the emerging form of post-Revolutionary urban society. From an individualistic, speculative, marvelously intricate trading pattern they must move to a systematically yet simply organized firm-based "business" pattern, dedicated to long-term economic ends. And from an interstitial, vaguely outcast position within traditional society they must move to an established place as respected shopkeepers and manufacturers, true bourgeois, within the developing class structure. Even more, they must do all this with sharply limited resources in a period of economic stagnation and political disorder, and in the face of intense competition from the Chinese, long entrenched as the most developed elements within the traditional economy. To say their chances are poor is thus simple realism; but then perhaps all major social changes appear impossible on the eve of their occurrence.

As noted, the social structure of the town as a whole is stalled in the middle of a transformation from a composite of self-contained and socially segregated status groups to a more broadly comprehensive set of across-the-board social classes. At the top of this hesitantly emerging class system are the leaders of the various political and quasi-political *aliran* organizations; at the bottom the steadily expanding urban proletariat. In between lies a quite loosely integrated collection of lower civil servants, school-teachers, small businessmen, skilled workers, petty professionals, technicians, clerks, and accountants who are coming to compose the sort of varigated, mixed-bag middle class which Modjokuto, up till now, has never had. Altogether the movement, vacillatory as it is, is toward a society at once less neatly outlined, less sharply stratified, and in a broad sense, less intensely religiously oriented; one in which the cultural trappings of traditional status are coming to count for less and the intellectual skills of modern education for more. It is upon the final establishment of such a society that the growth of a vigorous shopkeeping and manu-facturing business community depends, for it is only in such a society that it has a useful role to play.[12]

[12] This intimate relationship between a well-organized business community and a modernized urban social structure is, in fact, fairly clearly recognized, at

In the light of the theories of Max Weber concerning the role of Protestantism in stimulating the growth of a business community in the West, it is perhaps not wholly surprising that the leaders in the creation of such a community in Modjokuto are for the most part Reformist Moslems, for the intellectual role of Reform in Islam, in some ways, has approached that of Protestantism in Christianity.[13] Emphasizing that the systematic and untiring pursuit of worldly ends may be a religiously significant virtue of fundamental importance, Reformism, which swept the urban trading classes all over Java from 1912 to 1920, paved the way for the creation of a genuinely bourgeois ethic. By purifying Indonesian Islam of Hinduist and animist mystical and ritualistic accretions and focusing attention on dogma and morality, by severely criticizing the traditional aversion of the Moslem community to formal organization of any kind, and by substituting a progress-oriented self-determinism for the creed's classical fatalism, it injected a new dynamic into the *pasar* context. Chinese-owned enterprises aside, of the seven well-established modern stores in Modjokuto, six are run by Reform or Reform-influenced Moslems; of the two dozen or more small factories, all but three or four are in pious Moslem hands.[14]

Thus, as far as Modjokuto is concerned, economic development is tending to take, despite marked cultural differences, the classical

least on the commercial side, by the people of Modjokuto town themselves. They too — or many of them — distinguish between the *pasar* trading complex and the *toko* store complex, and they do so mainly in terms of contrast between "modern" (*moderen*) and "old-fashioned" (*kolot*). The *pasar*, they say, sells poorer quality goods to "village people," to the "ignorant" and "backward." "Those who know" trade mainly in the Javanese and Chinese stores of the town's business district. These latter prefer the more reliable, regularized atmosphere of the store to the hectic haggling of the market, and the inventory the stores carry — shoes, bicycles, manufactured furniture, ready-made clothing, etc. — is more directly adjusted to the Western-influenced revolution in tastes which the emerging urban classes are experiencing.

[13] Weber, *op. cit.*, The history of the Islamic Reform movement in Modjokuto is treated in detail in C. Geertz, *The Religion of Java* (Glencoe, Ill.: Free Press, 1960) pp. 131–61.

[14] The major exceptions to this generalization are a few stores and factories, run by members of the *prijaji* class. For a description of these see C. Geertz, "Religious Belief and Economic Behavior in a Central Javanese Town," *Economic Development and Cultural Change*, IV, No. 2 (1956), 134–58.

form we have known in the West: an at least in part religiously motivated, generally disesteemed group of small shopkeepers and petty manufacturers arising out of a traditional trading class is attempting to secure an improved status in a changing society — one in which the established barriers to mobility are weakening — through the rational, systematic pursuit of wealth. Occuring several centuries later than it did in Europe, in a world which is already partially industrialized, the significance and probable outcome of this particular sequence of change is of course quite different in Java. But that the similarity between the two cases is not wholly imaginary is evident from the following interview with the proprietor of one of Modjokuto's most successful Javanese-owned stores and largest garment factories, in which the ethos of this struggling entrepreneurial group finds a form of expression oddly reminiscent of the ideological pronouncements of the non-conformist businessmen of our own history:

He comes from Surabaja. His father was a tailor there before the war and taught him trading and tailoring. He has four brothers, all in trade, but in different towns and all on their own, completely independent economically.

I asked him what he thought the reason for his success was, especially since most Javanese don't do very well in business. He said it was very simple: all he does is work and pray, work and pray; and it only takes a few minutes to pray. His place is open from six A.M. to eleven P.M., seven days a week, and doesn't shut except for an hour or so around evening prayer. The only holiday he observes all year is Hari Raya [Idul Fitri; the day ending the Moslem fast month]. And, he said, when we are not selling we are working at something else. We are not like the people in the market who between their attempts to sell something just sit there and waste time. We work continually.

He only hires workers who are already mature, who have families and thus have many needs and want to work as hard as they can. Single people he won't touch; they just seek pleasure and the good life. It is better to have good stable married people who need the money and will work hard for it. He won't let his workers take a day off the job unless they have a good excuse, and as he has a great many people who want to work for him he doesn't need to fool around with people who are not serious. You can't allow unregulated absenteeisms, coming late to work, and still produce work on schedule. In his shop if you order something to be done in a week it will be done in a week, not in ten days, and the only way you can do this is by having an ordered shop. . . .

He rambled on, unprompted, saying there are two equal things in Islam: this world and the next, and nothing else, so that if you work hard and pray that's all you need do. I asked him about fate. He said that in his opinion everyone is given an even chance. Thus those who are poor are poor mainly because they are lazy, stupid, or sinful. For example, they gamble. While those who are rich are rich because they work hard and are clever. If he himself is well-off, for example, it is not from divine predestination but a result of his own efforts, and anyone could be the same if they would only try hard enough. It is, however, important to give thanks to God for one's good fortune.

The precise scope and quality of the organizational undertaking upon which this man and others like him are embarked in their effort to construct a firm economy out of a bazaar economy can best be understood by means of some concrete examples of their efforts. In general, these fall into two sorts: retail stores and small factories. Stores are called *toko* — originally a Chinese word; factories, *perusahaan* — an Indonesian word from *usaha*, "effort." I shall describe very briefly three *toko*, ranging from one which has still only partially escaped from the bazaar economy to one which is fully established along lines familiar to Westerners, and several *perusahaan*, showing a similar progression toward autonomous, firmlike organization.

THREE STORES

Along the front edge of the market place, the colonial government built, toward the end of the depression, a neat row of small, wood-and-plaster shops designed, as a welfare measure, to be rented to Javanese at a nominal cost. The intention was to create a second business district, rival to the older, Chinese-dominated one north of the public square and thus to stimulate the growth

of a native shopkeeper class. Today, most of these shops are in
Chinese hands and the program of economic reform through
building construction forgotten; but a few are still Javanese-
operated. One of these, Toko Kudus — so called because the young
man who runs it is a descendant of one of the leading trader
families migrant from this north coast area in the twenties — provides an excellent example of a store only partially differentiated
from the general market pattern out of which it has grown.

It is only partially differentiated in that rather than being a
separate, self-standing entity it — or its owner — is involved in a
vast complex of commercial ties with market-traders, independent
craftsmen, Chinese wholesalers, and the like, ties which are organized along the *ad hoc,* person-to-person, credit-balance lines
we have traced for the *pasar* generally. Some ten or so small circuit-
traders are more or less permanently dependent upon the proprietor, taking his textiles, hats, ready-made clothing, shawls, and
the like on credit and traveling out to the villages to sell them.
He supplies cloth to a small, local, hat manufacturer and provides
an outlet for the manufacturer's hats. His father is engaged in
putting out garment-making jobs to a large number of independent tailors working in their homes, and many of the shirts,
trousers, and underpants thus produced are sold in the store.
His uncle, his sister, several of his cousins, and assorted brothers-
in-law are all textile-traders in the *pasar,* and a complicated, ever
changing network of transactions relates his activities intimately
to theirs. Along with these relatives and a dozen or more substantial cloth-traders (all of them members of *Nahdatul Ulama,*
of whose youth organization the proprietor is the head) he belongs
to about the only effective textile buying co-operative in the *pasar,*
his store acting as the group's warehouse. In all this, selling
directly to the public still plays a relatively minor part, and in
essence Toko Kudus is little more than an elaborate market stall
with doors on it, a few glassed-in cases, and a sign in front.

Despite the fact that Toko Kudus is hardly a true store, its
owner regards himself as at least an aspirant shopkeeper, not a
mere glorified bazaar-trader, and he takes as his model not substantial market-oriented merchants such as his father or his uncle,

whom he regards as admirable but old-fashioned, but the larger, more established "businessmen" of the town, whose enterprises are more clearly autonomous. The major elements of the store pattern are, as a matter of fact, present here, if only in embryonic form: a permanent location, a full business day, somewhat more fixed prices, regular salesclerks, an adjustment of inventories to modern urban tastes, a more conscientious effort to carry out systematic bookkeeping-based planning, a more aggressive search for customers, and so on. If the young proprietor succeeds in accumulating capital through saving out of his increasing income, and adapts himself more and more carefully to the changing pattern of urban tastes, his store may develop along the lines the more established shops have followed, may move further along the continuum from *pasar* to *toko*. In this connection it is of some interest that during a brief revisit to Modjokuto three years after the original research in 1952–54, it was discovered that Toko Kudus had physically doubled in size, absorbing the neighboring shop, diversifying its inventory and increasing its emphasis on retail selling; clearly, it had become more than simply a convenient center for bazaar coalitions.

Our second, rather more developed store is that of the man who attributed his success to work and prayer and the fact that it took but a few minutes to pray. (An intense adherent of the *Masjumi aliran*, he fought in the Revolution in Hizbullah, the *Masjumi* guerilla army.) His store is also situated in the row of market-front buildings. In fact, he occupies two very large shops, one on either side of the main entrance to the market, in one of which he has a garment factory — so that his enterprise is both a *perusahaan* and a *toko* — and in the other an unusually attractive retail store. The proprietor is, in fact, the only shopkeeper in town, Javanese or Chinese, with a genuine flair for display merchandising. The shop, which is painted a bright green and displays the store's name, the owner's name, and that of his wife (advertised as a "modiste") has a glassed-in, awning-shaded, neon-lit display window in which there is an armless dummy clothed in Western dress, several styles of jackets for men, skirts for women, and dresses for little girls hanging from specially constructed racks, and well-planned layouts of shoes, socks, shawls, etc. In front of the window, bulk cloth is carefully arranged in eye-catching patterns on a clever fold-out shelf, and inside the store the merchandise — textiles, clothes, patent medicines, shoes, etc. — is set out in a half-dozen large glassed-in display cases, costing about the equivalent of $200 apiece. There are even a settee, several easy chairs, and a table where customers may sit. About all that is lacking in comparison with a typical small-town American shop of this sort is a cash register, and the abacus substitutes for that.

The heart of this enterprise is, of course, the garment factory; although the steadily increasing importance of the proprietor's agencies for Surabaja-made shoes, Chinese patent medicines, and Hong Kong–imported stockings is beginning to make his dependence on the manufacture of clothing less total. He employs from ten to fifteen tailors, according to the season, half of them women, producing both ready-made and custom-tailored clothing. (The custom clothes are generally cheaper, because less well-sewn and designed than the ready-made; custom-making is the traditional pattern, ready-mades the modern.) They work on machines owned by the proprietor, on a piecework basis, and, as noted, he works them very long hours. About 50 per cent of the cost of a jacket, pair of trousers, or dress, he estimated roughly, goes to the workers, about 20 per cent goes for the material, about 10 per cent for rent and equipment, 10 per cent for designing, marking, and cutting (which he, his father, or his wife does), allowing a profit of 10 per cent. All in all, he says he grosses from three to five thousand rupiah a month — although I have no independent check of the accuracy of this estimate — which would yield a good but not spectacular income for Modjokuto.

The store's clientele consists mainly of the more urbanized "middle classes" of the town as well as the more town-influenced village people — those who, as the proprietor puts it, "know a little." In his estimate, perhaps 80 per cent of his customers are regular, and he is conscious in his effort to build a stable market, an established local reputation. For example, all his garments are double-sewn, and this, he says, is an excellent selling point to

people who want something just a little better than the shabby
ready-made clothes one finds in the market. (The prices of his
garments run perhaps 10 to 20 per cent above those of *pasar*-
produced clothing.)[15] For this reason too, the proprietor refuses
to sell through the agency of *pasar* traders, gives out no goods on
a credit-balance arrangement, and almost all of his sales are retail.
Only poorer quality goods can be sold effectively through *pasar*
traders, he claims, and in any case, theses traders, who go from
deal to deal, do not worry at all about reputation. He fears that
in their eagerness to cut corners they may damage his hard-won
reputation for reliability. Bazaar-traders also often dirty the goods
or damage them, which makes little difference if the merchandise
is cheap anyway; but his better quality merchandise is not salable
if it is not clean and undamaged. The great majority of the people
around Modjokuto still want only the poorer quality market
clothes, which can be sold efficiently through the circuit-traders,
but an increasing number of people today desire something a
little more "advanced," and these usually either live in town or
are willing to walk in if they know they can get what they want.

On the buying side there is a similar contraction of trade ties:
unlike the more substantial textile-traders in the *pasar*, who for
the most part journey to the large cities of Surabaja, Surakarta,
or Kediri, or to nearby towns to purchase their materials, the
proprietor buys everything he needs from the local Chinese or
from agents of city-based companies who come to Modjokuto.
Wholesale prices in Modjokuto are, of course, noticeably higher
than in the large cities, but he calculates that his time is too
valuable to make the trips away from work — the extended shop-
ping around, the protracted bargaining, and the multiple and
complicated transactions involved — economic. As against the bazaar pattern, therefore, this store represents not only a far more
consistent effort to seek out and stimulate customers, to exploit
a developing market, but, perhaps even more crucially, it also
represents a radical simplification of the distributive apparatus,

[15] In general, prices slide less in this store than in the bazaar, but they are
still not totally fixed. People, especially those from the villages, simply won't
believe in completely fixed prices, the proprietor insists; if you won't bargain,
they won't buy.

a rationalized regularization of the flow of goods between producer and consumer. Its primary innovational contribution lies,
once again, in the field of organization.

The third store lies not in the row of market-front shops but
in the main business district northward, wedged in among the
Chinese *toko*, and it is the most fully developed Javanese-owned
store in Modjukuto. It is also the oldest. Founded and still managed by a Hadji (i.e., a Meccan pilgrim) who is at the same time
secretary and general guardian angel of *Muhammadijah*, the main
Reformist association in town, the store was established in 1931,
at the point at which the sugar boom was just beginning to taper
off. The proprietor is the son of a prosperous storekeeper in
Madiun, a large central Javanese town some seventy miles west
of Modjokuto, where the boom in plantation agriculture also
stimulated indigenous commercial expansion in the twenties. As
they came of age, this man sent each of the sons out to found a
store with capital provided by him. In such a way, four more or
less identical *toko* were set up in the east-central Javanese towns
of Blitar, Telungagung, Kediri, and Modjokuto, each store having
the same name as that owned by the father (Toko Ibrahim, after
the Moslem prophet), and all thrived. But despite the apparent
"chain" quality of these shops, their proprietors became wholly
independent of one another and of the father who had launched
them (and to whom they had repaid their debts) within only a
few years, and the development of each Toko Ibrahim has followed an autonomous course since.

For Modjokuto's Toko Ibrahim, the high point of this development took place in the prewar period. At this time, it approached
the largest Chinese drygoods stores in size, diversity of inventory,
and volume of sales. The store sold household equipment, canned
and other prepared foods, various sorts of hardware, stationery —
the whole great number of things one finds in a rural "general
store" almost anywhere in the world. Since the Revolution, the
scale of the Hadji's business has contracted somewhat, but at the
same time he has also adapted it more exactly to the concurrent
revolution in urban tastes. Today he sells sports equipment (bad-
minton, Ping-pong, and tennis rackets, soccer balls, athletic sup-

porters), toys (miniature trucks, wooden machine guns, a fantastic line of dolls with bright red hair and blue eyes), scarves and table cloths decorated with pictures of President Sukarno or shadow-play heroes, various sorts of modern clothing including pith helmets, overseas caps, and rain hats; cigarettes, perfume, fountain pens, parasols, flashlights, books (mostly on Islamic subjects, but some popular magazines as well), brief cases, women's purses, bicycle decorations, a line of attractively packaged Chinese medicines and rice wines; and so on through the whole range of the sumptuary symbols of modern urban life. The real heart of the Hadji's enterprise, however, is his agency for Bata shoes, secured just after the end of the war.[16] Of these he stocks well over five hundred pairs and sells more than two hundred pairs a month, at about Rp. 40 each — in itself a measure of the revolution in urban (and urbanized village) living. At a 10 per cent rate of commission this in itself yields an excellent income by Modjokuto standards, and, combined with the profits from his other lines, it makes the Hadji one of the town's wealthiest Javanese.

Despite its vicissitudes, Toko Ibrahim represents, therefore, the clearest example of the development of a true store out of the general *pasar* context. Oriented to the emerging urban market, based on an activist, regularized, systematic approach to business, and specialized in retail selling, it points the direction in which the renovation of Modjokuto distributive apparatus must move if genuine economic take-off is ever to occur. In discussions of economic growth, the emphasis on the mechanization of industry and agriculture, certainly essential elements in any attempt to raise per capita income in such a country as Indonesia, has often obscured the concurrent necessity for reform in the system of distribution and the contribution to development such

[16] The Bata shoe concern, originally Czechoslovakian, has pioneered in Indonesia in the mass retailing of domestically manufactured cheap shoes through hundreds of small, Indonesian-owned outlets. The shoes are dispatched by mail and sold on commission, and form a "bread-and-butter" line upon which various sorts of small shops all over Indonesia rely. Bata has thus probably contributed more to stimulating small-scale local entrepreneurship than any other foreign-owned company in Indonesia.

reform can make in and of itself. "Bata's" contribution to Indonesia's economy for the past several decades has been not simply the production of a cheap, relatively durable shoe — other companies, even local handicraft, can and do compete in these terms — but in creating a simple, reliable distributive system for their shoes which, relying on the mails and hundreds of petty agents, is adjusted to the local situation and includes local business and local businessmen as an essential part.

The success of Javanese stores in breaking new ground outside the traditional routines of trade seems, in fact, to be heavily dependent upon the possibility of establishing workable relations with stable, reliable distributors on the one side, to complement the growth of similar relations with the emerging urban public on the other. With a few mainstays of this sort, whether shoes, or patent medicines, or ready-made clothes, the storekeeper can, like the proprietor of Toko Ibrahim, experiment more easily along less settled and predictable lines. Nor is the value of such a relationship confined to the sort of dry goods stores we have been describing. A large local grocer capitalized his innovations in food selling by means of a permanent tie with a producer of lime (for whitewash) in southern Java, managing to dispose of nearly a truckload a day. The expansion of a bicycle store — the owner added awnings, glass display cases, advertising signs, and two employees in the space of a few months — was made possible by a relationship to a supplier in the regional capital, who permitted the owner to sell parts and bicycles on a commission basis. And the local bookstore had most of its stock on consignment from publishers. A sustained transition to economic growth in an underdeveloped country demands a commercial revolution as much as it demands an industrial and an agricultural revolution. The *pasar* stands as much in the way of Indonesian economic progress as does machineless handicraft and overintensive cultivation; the significance of the sort of *toko* development here traced lies in the fact that it charts, so far as Modjokuto is concerned, one of the most important and most immediate avenues of escape from the inefficiency of the underorganized, overcomplicated bazaar economy.

CRAFTWORK AND MANUFACTURING

Aside from the differentiation of more highly organized commercial firms, or *toko*, out of the general bazaar background, there is as well a similar differentiation of manufacturing firms, or *perusahaan*. These latter, however, grow most directly out of the handicraft rather than the trading aspects of the traditional *pasar* (though the two usually cannot be very sharply discriminated from one another in actual practice): parallel to the continuum from bazaar-trader to store-proprietor, there is a similar continuum from bazaar craftsman to factory manager. For this reason, it is necessary, as a first step toward understanding small industry in Modjokuto, to look for a moment at the traditional Javanese craftsmen — his skills, his resources, and his manner of work.

The Javanese (and Indonesian) word for craftsman is *tukang*. This term can be applied to almost anyone who has a particular occupational skill of any sort. *Besi* is iron, a *tukang besi* is a smith. *Djahit* is to sew, *tukang djahit* is a tailor. *Potong* is to cut, a *tukang potong* is either a barber, a butcher, or a circumciser; sometimes all three. The nearly infinite number of skills whose pratitioners can be called *tukangs* is remarked by the Javanese themselves when they refer, ironically, to a corrupt politician as a *tukang korsi* (*korsi* — chair, seat; and, by extension, parliamentary seat); a long-winded speaker as a *tukang omong kosong* (*omong* — to talk; *kosong* — empty); or a Don Juan as a *tukang main perumpuan* (*main* — to play; *perumpuan* — woman). Bricklayers, carpenters, cobblers, goldsmiths, potters, cigarette-rollers, various sorts of food-preparers, mat and basket-weavers — and nowadays, watchmakers and bicycle repairmen — are other types of independent and self-sufficient skilled workers falling under the general rubric of *tukang*. For our purposes, however, the crafts of carpenter and tailor may serve as examples both of typically individuated *tukang* operation, and of the ways in which more highly organized firm-type forms of productive activity are slowly growing up in the industries traditionally served by such handicraft.

The traditional town carpenter uses his home as his workshop. Generally, he is engaged in several sorts of activity: the hand-sawing of timber to make lumber; the construction of cheap and simple furniture — tables, chairs, bedsteads, and cupboards; and the repairing or building of small, village and proletarian-type bamboo shacks. All of these tasks he can fairly easily accomplish by himself, perhaps with the aid of a young, often unpaid, apprentice.[17] He makes his own tools, seeks his own wood, does all his work, even furniture-making, on an individual, prepaid, made-to-order contract basis, and finds his jobs by keeping his eyes and ears open and importuning his friends and acquaintances. Sometimes he is overwhelmed with work; more often, especially now that dozens of destitute former plantation workers have flooded the occupation, he goes for weeks with nothing to do. Separated from the manual laborer class only by his slowly acquired skill and experience, the average carpenter lives a life and occupies a status more or less comparable to that of the average petty trader.

The carpenters' traditional individualistic mode of operation first becomes inadequate in relation to the construction of the wood, brick, cement, and plaster Dutch-style bungalows which have rapidly become the mode among established urban classes in the years since World War II. Here (as well as in the erection of modern business establishments, government offices, etc.), not only must brickmakers, plasterers, carpenters, and electricians be integrated into a fairly complex yet carefully co-ordinated productive effort, but the carpentry work in itself is of too complicated and extended a character to permit one man to undertake it alone. The result has been the rise of a compromise form of labor organization called the *stel* or "set" system, which preserves the independence of the individual *tukang* and yet permits him to co-operate with other *tukang* in a given productive process.

A *stel*, or set, consists of any one of three combinations of

[17] The framework of any building, even a modern one, is for ritual reasons, still inevitably raised, in one sustained effort, by a "working bee" party of friends, relatives, and neighbors of the owner. This sort of communal labor, called *saja*, has disappeared from all other aspects of urban life, but it is still sometimes employed in the villages for various tasks.

workers: either (1) two craftsmen (e.g., both of them carpenters, or both bricklayers); or (2) three unskilled manual laborers (called *buruh* as distinct from *tukang*); or, (3) one craftsman plus two manual laborers. Such sets represent relatively lasting arrangements. The two craftsmen, or the single craftsman and his two unskilled helpers who form a set, will tend always to work together whenever an opportunity for employment on a larger building project appears. (For normal work they continue, of course, to operate wholly independently.)

The way the system works is as follows. One craftsman, usually a somewhat better-off and well-known carpenter or bricklayer, will receive the contract from the client in jobbing form: for a certain, well-haggled sum he undertakes to build the house, store, office, or whatever. This man is the *anémer*, from the Dutch word for "contractor." In line with Javanese notions of the behavior proper to a leader, he will, however, perform none of the actual construction work himself, even though he is a *tukang*. Rather, he seeks however many sets of carpenters, bricklayers, and laborers he feels he needs. For the average bungalow he may need one, two-*tukang* set of bricklayers, two, three-man manual laborer sets to carry bricks and mix cement for them and perform other menial tasks, and perhaps two or three of the one carpenter plus two laborers type of sets, each of which will be assigned fully separate and distinct tasks in the actual job of building. Each of these sets is also hired on a lump-sum jobbing basis, and the dimensions of their particular tasks are quite precisely and exclusively defined. The contractor is responsible for seeing that the work follows the plan, and that the various sets do their work, receive their just rewards, and keep out of one another's way. In organizational terms, the point to be grasped is that in the *stel* system stable work-associations occur only in the elements which make up the crew, not in the crew as a whole. The sets remain more or less fixed from job to job, but which sets are working with which on any one job is, if not entirely random, at least highly variable.

The final stage to date in this evolution toward firm organization of the carpentry trade in Modjokuto is the fairly recent establishment of four or five permanently staffed Javanese-owned "sawmills," called *geradjèn*. A sawmill is owned by a single carpenter, but anywhere from one or two to a half-dozen sets of craftsmen and laborers are also to a greater or lesser degree regularly employed there. Such a sawmill integrates the three main productive operations of the traditional carpenter into a single, compound enterprise. Most of the time of the laborer sets is spent in pit-sawing of timber into lumber, for which they are paid by the board foot.[18] The craftsmen spend their days making furniture out of some of this lumber, on a piecework basis, and, unlike the individual carpenter, the sawmill owner is able to produce furniture which has not yet been contracted for and so keep the various sets working more continuously. And when an opportunity to build a modern house, store, or office appears, the proprietor of the sawmill can cease lumber-making and furniture-building operations temporarily and employ his craftsman and laborer sets to this end.[19] Particularly with the growth of modern governmental building programs — housing, schools, offices — several of these permanently established *anémers* have been able to build up fairly sizable and stable construction, milling, and furniture businesses, escaping almost altogether from the bazaar economy pattern.

A somewhat similar development from craftsman to businessman has occurred in the garment-making trades. Again, the overwhelming bulk of the production which takes place in Modjokuto is still carried out by lone, independent craftsmen working in their homes (though a few tailors set up stalls in the market place proper.) Unlike the carpentry trade, however, tailoring demands a significant initial investment of about seven hundred to a thousand *rupiah* — three or four months income for an average tailor — to buy a sewing machine, so that the profession is a little less overcrowded. These tailors — almost each one of whom has a showy white sport jacket hanging in the window of his house as a symbol of his trade — work entirely on a to-order basis. The customer purchases the necessary cloth in the market and brings

[18] This is the most readily mechanized of the woodworking processes, but so far only two sawmill owners have grown prosperous enough to purchase motor-driven rotary saws.

[19] The bricklaying must, however, still be contracted for separately by the proprietor.

it to the tailor to be made into a jacket, a pair of trousers, a blouse, or whatever. Here, too, the work cycle of the individual craftsman oscillates violently and unpredictably between periods of frenetic activity and periods of absolute idleness; and to see a tailor promenading about in his white jacket in the early evening (hardly anyone ever actually purchases so extravagant a jacket for himself) is to surmise that economically he is about to give up, sell his machine and his jacket, and return to petty trade in textiles.

The first level of more intensive organization of the garment-making industry can be seen in the putting-out system, which remains very widespread in Java generally. This system operates in Modjokuto in about the same manner as it does in other underdeveloped countries, and as it did in medieval Europe, with about the same severe exploitation of the petty craftsman by the middleman engrosser. Most engrossers are textile-traders and tailors at the same time. They buy the cloth, cut it to design, and then farm it out to individual tailors to sew, after which they sell the finished garment in the *pasar*. For example, one man, also a leading Reform Moslem, is engaged wholly in the putting-out manufacture of brassières. He has eight women working for him (on the average; seasonal variations are large in putting-out garment work), each on her own machine in her own home. He travels to Surabaja once in ten days to buy cloth, which he marks in the correct pattern and gives out to the seamstresses, who, working from dawn to well past dusk, and usually aided by one or two of their daughters or nieces to hand-sew the buttons, can produce about 150 brassières a day among them. Such a worker will earn, at the most, about Rp. 50 a week, barely a living wage, while the net profit to the engrosser, who sells the finished brassières to about a half-dozen market traders on a stable credit-balance arrangement, will run perhaps two or three times that much. This method in essentially the same — although sometimes even more oppressive — form is used to manufacture trousers, underwear, shirts, and blouses. In all there are more than a dozen such enterprises in Modjokuto, of which the largest employs up to fifteen tailors at peak periods.

The transition from bazaar to firm organization occurs, however, in the establishment of true garment factories, where the tailors work regular hours on machines owned by the proprietor, in a shop provided by him, and under his direct guidance. We have mentioned one example of such organization in connection with one of Modjokuto's retail stores, and there are three or four more, roughly comparable, examples of such autonomous factories in the town. The major advantage of such factory organization is that it permits a greater rationalization of production because it allows the work process to be divided up in a more analytic manner: rather than three men each making an entire shirt in the privacy of their individual homes, one man can make the sleeves, cuffs, and collars, a second can make the rest, and a third can assemble the parts and sew on the buttons in a production-line arrangement. On the other hand, this sort of technical integration (which in the garment industry has a strong tendency, particularly in the absence of labor unions, to lead to sweatshop conditions) demands much greater discipline on the part of the workers, for they must adjust both the speed and the style of their work to one another so that the separately manufactured pieces will be available when needed. Modjokuto tailors draw a fairly clear line between "modern" craftsmen who can follow a pattern accurately and speedily enough to operate effectively in a factory setting, and "old-fashioned" ones — by far the great majority — who cannot, and so must work alone, either independently or in a putting-out arrangement.

As a specimen of factory organization in the garment trade, we may take the Airship Hat Factory, so called because the label placed in the hats happens to show a four-motored airplane.[20] The factory is owned by two young men, both members of important Moslem commercial families, one a twenty-five-year-old tailor, the other a twenty-three-year-old textile-trader, and employs seven tailors (also all young men and all pious Moslems) on five ma-

[20] Modern Western symbols are universally favored as trade-marks in such concerns. A very common practice is to take well-known American trade-marks and apply them to goods of a sort wholly different from those with which they are properly associated, so that you get General Motors shirts, Ford socks, and, as a classic in the genre, Frigidaire underpants.

chines owned, borrowed, or rented by the proprietors. The
industry began on the proverbial shoestring with two machines
into a few hundred rupiahs' worth of cloth, and initially was
engaged in the rather haphazard manufacture of cheap overseas
hats of the sort symbolically associated with the nationalist movement in Indonesia. Soon, however, a Chinese factory in a nearby
town began selling such hats at less than what it cost Airship to
make them. The owners then switched to flimsy white caps of the
kind Chinese schoolboys wear in Indonesia, but the market for
these was too restricted to stimulate much growth. One day, the
tailor-proprietor saw a Western-type "bucket" hat, imported from
Hong Kong, in a Chinese store in Modjokuto, bought it, took it
home, took it apart, and traced out the pattern, and the partners
decided they could make such a hat themselves and undersell
Hong Kong. In this they have been eminently successful, for the
factory now produces, assembly-line fashion, about two hundred
such hats (one hundred in each of two sizes) a week, netting about
Rp. 100 for each of the entrepreneurs, with about Rp. 60 for each
of the tailors.

That this factory has left the bazaar economy largely behind it
and resolutely entered the firm economy is apparent from its
dealings with the larger concerns from which it gets its raw materials and to which it sells its product. For the first year or so
of operation, Airship bought all its cloth from the largest Chinese
store in Modjokuto and disposed of 90 per cent of its hats to the
same store, and thus existed more or less on the sufferance of this
established concern. Convinced, however, that they were receiving
an unjustly low price for their wares, they "went on strike,"
refusing to sell any more hats to this Chinese store. Buying cloth
elsewhere, they began to sell their hats, for a slightly higher price,
to a Pakistani storekeeper in a town some thirty or forty miles
away, even though the additional transportation costs not only
wiped out any gain for these young businessmen but actually cut
their profit margin. In the end, the local Chinese store capitulated
and met the price of the Pakistani competition, and the old relationship was restored, although a lesser percentage of the total
output was now funneled through this single outlet. In their

aggressive unwillingness simply to accept the status quo as divinely given, in their ability to play off one businessman (and one national group) against another, and in the vigor with which they carried their plan through to a successful conclusion, the hat manufacturers demonstrated quite clearly that, given any luck at all, they could survive and prosper in a more demanding and more rewarding economic environment than that provided by the traditional bazaar.

HOUSEHOLD INDUSTRY AND MANUFACTURING

Not all of Modjokuto's small industries are evolutions out of a traditional craftsman, *tukang* context, of course; some — like brickmaking, cigarette-rolling, potting, food-processing, basket-weaving, or charcoal-manufacturing — though of long-standing importance as village crafts, have always been carried out in a non-professional, part-time manner which did not demand the creation of definite, specialized roles to perform them.[21] Modernization, here, is not so much a matter of organizing traditionally institutionalized craft roles into more complex patterns as of transforming an essentially secondary and subsidiary household industry pattern into a full-time factory form of productive organization. As examples of this sort of industrial pattern in Modjokuto, we may look briefly first at a small cluster of bean-curd factories, where the household industry element is still prominent; and, second, at a partially mechanized sugar factory, where it has been left almost completely behind.

In the southeast section of Modjokuto, immediately behind the line of Chinese stores, there is a typical between-the-streets cluster of shabby, lower-class bamboo shacks, known in this case as the "Bean-curd Neighborhood," because within this group of perhaps fifty families there are five bean-curd factories, with which probably almost all of the resident adults are involved in one way or another. The first of these factories was erected in 1920 by a

---

[21] There are no weaving industries in Modjokuto at all, nor do there seem to have been any for many years, with the exception of the Japanese occupation period when the complete disruption of imports led to some small-scale textile manufacturing in the villages.

woman who, evidently, had learned the craft working for a Modjokuto Chinese. One by one, the other four factories appeared, founded by neighborhood people who had, in turn, worked for this pioneer, until the Chinese, who once monopolized the entire trade, were largely driven from it by Javanese competition.

This highly unusual and peculiar triumph of Javanese enterprises over Chinese seems to have been due largely to the fact that there are few, if any, economies of scale in the bean-curd industry: not much capital is needed and even very small factories can operate profitably; and in such a way a cluster of small shops can run one large one out of business simply by keeping labor costs to a minimum. Like the *stel* system in house-building, and the putting-out system in garment-making, the bean-curd industry represents only a first and partial step away from the bazaar pattern as it appears on the processing rather than on the distributive side of traditional commerce.

Bean-curd, a small piece of which most Javenese eat with every meal, and which is probably their main source of protetin, is made from soya bean, which is grown as a major dry season crop around Modjokuto. The beans are soaked in water for about six hours until they become mushy. They are then ground between one fixed stone and one movable one, the movable one being rotated by hand through an ingenious spindle-and-pulley arrangement suspended from the ceiling. The result of this operation, which may take a half-hour or so, is a semiliquid pulp which is then screened for major impurities and cooked in a large vat for several hours. This cooking is an attention-demanding job because the pulp must be added gradually, can by can, and must be stirred continually. While still boiling, the cooked product is now screened again, this time through a piece of cheesecloth stretched over a vat, and vinegar is added to cause the by now milk-like substance to curdle. The separated liquid is siphoned off, and the curds are placed on a bamboo tray to dry in the sun, this whole straining, siphoning, and curdling process taking perhaps ten or fifteen minutes. When, in about an hour, the curds are dry, or reasonably so, they are carefully molded into squares through a process of enclosing them in a small piece of cloth and dextrously folding the cloth into a flattened cube. Next, the little patties thus formed are pressed even dryer with a flat board, and then they are fried in deep fat for about a half-hour. Finally they are wrapped separately in paper for sale; and this, as bean curd does not keep, must take place within a day or two of manufacture.

As can be seen from this compressed and generalized description, the productive process of the bean-curd industry is one particularly suited to a bazaar economy. First, the capital investment required is small — about five hundred rupiah in all, or less than most tailors pay for their sewing machines — and marginal increases in capital investment are not in themselves likely to lead to any greater efficiency. When you have your grinder and your cooking vat you are in business, and aside from simple physical expansion — two grinders and two cooking vats — you can hardly improve upon your initial position, especially since profit margins and labor costs are already so low that incremental investments in equipment improvement are not likely to be economic. Second, the productive process is divisible into small, more or less separate and only loosely integrated parts — grinding, squeezing, straining, boiling, molding, frying, and wrapping — none of which demands any great amount of skill, though some need care and diligence. This permits irregular operation, extreme flexibility in organization, and a high degree of sensitivity to market conditions on the part of the factory as a unit. Because almost anyone can do any job, and because there is nothing about the process which necessitates continuous operation beyond the production of a single "batch" of bean-curd (which, in itself, can vary greatly in size), people may come and go more or less freely, working when they wish to and being replaced by others of the neighborhood when they do not. And, for the same reasons, the manufacturing process itself can vary from almost continuous day-and-night operation in rush periods, as before a great holiday or after the harvest, to very sporadic operation — a batch now, another two or three days from now — in quieter periods. In fact, almost every man, woman, and child in the neighborhood over the age of nine or ten spends some time each month in manufacturing bean-curd, but none draws a full-time living from it.

And, third, both the purchase of raw materials and the sale of output can be executed quite effectively through the traditional bazaar mechanisms. Soya beans can be bought basket by basket in the *pasar* as the need arises, and the finished curds may be sold, square by square, to *pasar* traders, on a typical credit-balance arrangement, as they are produced.

These three factors — low fixed costs, a generally invertebrate technical structure, and integration into the hyperflexible marketing system of the bazaar — make possible a still semitraditional manufacturing pattern in which the role of the entrepreneur is not sharply differentiated from that of the generalized, part-time handicraft role on the one hand or that of the market-trader on the other. Rather than five well-defined factories, each with a proprietor who purchases materials, directs the work, and sells the product, what you have here, actually, are five "plants" — each, to be sure, owned by a different individual — within which a certain manufacturing process takes place through the agency of an almost continually changing personnel and leadership. If the owner of such a plant wishes to, he may, of course, buy some soya beans, hire some workers, and produce some bean-curd; but so may just about anyone else of standing in the neighborhood. Anyone with the capital to buy beans may rent one of the plants for a very nominal sum (or perform some counterfavor for the owner) in order to produce the curd. You may direct the work yourself, or you may get someone else to do it. You may participate in the production yourself, sometimes in the most unskilled activity, sometimes directing it, or you may not, simply handling the trading end. Sometimes one man may be providing capital (and/or productive effort) for two or three factories at once; sometimes two or three men may be pooling capital to operate one. And so on. Although one or two of the factories are in operation most of the time, who is working in them, who is providing the capital, and who is directing the work vary from month to month, even from week to week. Certain individuals, of course, consistently play a more important role than others, and not everyone is equally skilled on either the processing or the distributing sides. But there is no fixed and settled firm-type factory organization. Rather, there is the sort of compromise, half-firm, half-bazaar pattern we have seen to be characteristic of the initial stages of modernization in all aspects of Modjokuto's economy.

In general, traditional household industries of the bean-curd sort are similar in essence to traditional agriculture: they are highly labor intensive, subject to wide seasonal fluctuations in activity, essentially loose and undynamic in their organization, and, because of the dwarf scale on which they operate, very difficult to capitalize effectively. In the village context, such industries are in fact usually treated as an adjunct to farming: when things are slow in the fields, activity picks up in brick-making, coconut oil manufacturing, or basket-weaving; and vice versa. Such household industries are viewed as additional cash crops, ones whose "growing seasons" can be inserted in between those of the ordinary crops to give a better balance to the yearly round. The result is an approach to manufacturing which is interested less in steadily increasing efficiency or in continually rising wages and profits than it is in a reliable, riskless source of supplemental income, in return for the irregular application of otherwise idle unskilled labor. Despite their urban setting, despite their somewhat larger scale and less subsidiary role in the people's economy, and despite their broader territorial rather than narrowly familial framework of organization, the factories of the bean-curd neighborhood have only just begun to escape this orientation: lacking any impulse toward a fundamental social and technical reorganization of the production process itself, they reduce urban underemployment but they do not stimulate urban reconstruction.

That household industry of this sort can be developed into a more advanced pattern is evident enough from one of Modjokuto's most highly mechanized factories, which produces the brown, unrefined cane sugar known traditionally as "Javanese sugar" (*gula djawa*), as opposed to the white, refined sugar known as "Dutch sugar" (*gula landa*), produced by the capital-intensive Dutch mills. The manufacture of Javanese sugar, which has gone on for centuries in Java, employs a productive process basically very like that for bean-curd: there is a similar squeezing, boiling,

A secondary
business street,
Modjokuto

Bookstore
run by
a modernist Moslem,
Modjokuto

A Modjokuto shopkeeper
who is also
a Meccan pilgrim (*hadji*)
and a modernist Moslem

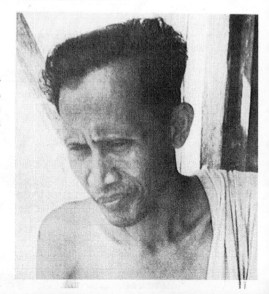

A Modjokuto carpenter (*Tukang kuju*) at work in a shop behind his home

Main street, Tabanan

Capping a tire in a factory owned by a prince, Tabanan. The worker is one of the prince's traditional dependents.

Balinese village women setting off for the town market

A morning market in a small Balinese village

Balinese musical instrument (*gamelan*) makers forging a large gong. The work group consists entirely of members of one patrilineal descent group.

treating, drying, and packaging of a field-grown, seasonal food crop; and the equipment of the household industry shop is also of about the same order — a grinder, a cooking vat, a drying tub, and so on. In the villages, the usual part-time, family-centered small-scale manner of production is still the mode, and marketing takes place in the ordinary bazaar, piece-by-piece style. Though sugar has an advantage over bean-curd in that it is less perishable, there seems little reason why, in itself, the small-scale production of unrefined, locally consumed sugar should be more susceptible to mechanization than many other household industries.

Modjokuto's mechanized "Javanese sugar" factory is owned by a small landlord and political leader and is run by a man who was for a short time a technician in a Dutch sugar mill, with a Chinese accountant to keep the books. It includes two sugar-cane pressing machines made in the large central Javanese city of Sura-karta, driven by two three-horsepower electro-motors manufac-tured in Japan. There is also a four-horsepower electro-diesel engine hooked to a third press, which is in turn mounted on a movable cart. The third, diesel-driven presser is used only from five P.M. until midnight when, because of the great load on the town's dynamos at this time, the factory is not permitted enough electricity to run the ordinary presses. Two men sit above the pressers, dropping stripped cane into them. Juice flows from the bottom through a trough to an open vat (the pressed cane emerges under the press and is used, after drying, as fuel for the cooking oven), where it is boiled and mixed with lime as a fixative. After this, the liquid is poured into a tub in which there is a large ro-tating wooden rake pivoted on a central wooden column, with handles extending over the edge of the tub at either end. The sugar cools and crystallizes as this rake is pushed manually around in a circle by about four men, after which it is sacked.

The whole process takes seven or eight hours, and the factory runs day and night in a more or less continuous operation, pro-ducing in one day and night around twelve quintals of sugar from about twelve metric tons of cane. Cane is bought from peas-ants who either bring it to the factory themselves or sell it to traders who buy it up and bring it in, and all the sugar is sold to a single Chinese who comes each day with a truck to haul it away. For the purely capitalist owner (whose investment runs somewhere around Rp. 15,000) the daily net profit, exclusive of depreciation, probably comes to about forty rupiah, which, as the factory runs seven days a week, represents a handsome income by Modjokuto standards.

The work in the factory is organized in four gangs of ten men, each of which operates on a jobbing basis. Each gang produces a single batch of sugar from pressing to sacking, and there is no fixed division of labor within the gang — each worker performs in turn each task as equity and the situation demands. Thus, each gang works for about eight hours and is paid — every ten days — as a whole, by the quintal of sugar they produce, the money thus received being divided equally among all the members of the gang and coming to about six or seven rupiah per worker per day. The reason that there are four shifts, rather than three, is that when one shift gets into the later phases of the process, the very tedious and back-breaking job of rake-stirring and crystallizing, the next shift may begin the earlier phases of pressing and boiling.[22] Thus, in ideal terms, you get an overlapping pattern such as the following, though in fact the variations in the length of time the process takes, and the general lack of necessity for precise scheduling, make the actual pattern less regular:

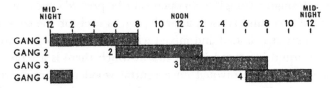

All in all, though simple by any definition, this is clearly firm organization, and everything about the factory gives the impression that it is well and systematically run: there is a large board with numbered tags, one for each worker, which acts as a sort of time clock, for the worker posts his number when he comes in

[22] In addition to the work gangs there are two salaried workers — at five rupiah a day — who merely tend the machines in alternate twelve-hour shifts, as well as a salaried sweeper and a man who strips cane. And, as mentioned above, over-all supervision is provided by a salaried technician.

and takes it down when he leaves; there is a toolboard with images of the tools painted on it for correct hanging; all the workers wear uniform denim clothing and most have worked several years in the mill. The sugar-milling season only lasts about seven months and in the off season the motors are turned to lumber-milling with a rotary saw, as a hedge against the high — for Modjokuto — fixed costs of the plant. Clearly, the entrepreneur, who is planning to found a rice mill and a construction concern as well, has taken the manufacture of Javanese sugar out of the realm of household and handicraft industry into that of the modern, mechanized factory.

A Rising Middle Class and its Problems

Modjokuto's fitful and sporadic movements toward economic reform are only part of her more general movement, also fitful and sporadic, toward a whole new pattern of social life; the search for novel forms of economic organization is only one aspect of a wider search for a fresh approach to over-all social and cultural integration. The movement from territorially based traditional political allegiances toward ideologically based modern ones in the *aliran* parties and associations, the transformation of the system of stratification from a collection of discrete, more or less closed status groups to across-the-board, culturally heterogeneous open classes, and the development of corporate economic firms out of a background of hyperindividuated bazaar trading are all of a piece. Each of these changes needs the others for it to flourish, and together they both produce and are the results of fundamental alterations in cultural beliefs, attitudes, and values. It is in this sense that such often vaguely employed terms as "modernization," "urbanization," "rationalization," and "economic development" are really equivalent in their basic meaning, for they all point, if from somewhat different standpoints, to an integral pattern of social change.

Yet this does not mean that the pattern is anywhere and everywhere the same, nor, under the generalization "everything is related to everything else," does it obviate the necessity of tracing its specific interrelations. Modjokuto's sequence of economic development has its own specificity, its own internal structure, which must be understood before its theoretical and practical significance, when seen against other specific sequences elsewhere, can be determined.

The first specific characteristic of Modjokuto's economic development is that it is occurring within and on the basis of a traditional trading pattern. The role of preindustrial trading groups in the transition to sustained growth has been much mooted in the literature on development, with some scholars arguing that traditional trade is not only not functional to the rise of the "modern capitalism" but actually inhibitory of it, and others arguing that it is the main source and dynamic in the evolution of modern economic institutions. Whatever its eventual role in Modjokuto, the bazaar pattern at the moment both facilitates and inhibits economic reform: it is both the context out of which the innovating elements are emerging and the confine against which they are struggling. Modjokuto's entrepreneurs are almost all traders or traders' sons, and both their strengths and their weaknesses derive from that fact.

The second characteristic is that the central problems the leaders in development face are organizational. Lack of capital, shortages of skilled or disciplined labor, insufficiency of markets, lack of technical knowledge, and so on are all, to some extent, genuine problems. But none of these seems in any proper sense an immediately limiting factor on economic development in contemporary Modjokuto, though they all might soon become so if that development were suddenly to accelerate. It is the ability and originality to organize a range of diverse economic activities into a unified institution — store or small factory — that most distinguishes a Modjokuto entrepreneur from his non-innovative bazaar-trader fellows, not wealth, not education, or even drive.

The third characteristic is that the entrepreneurial group is a group, not a random collection of individuals. Modjokuto's innovators are set apart both by their social origins and by their religious intensity; they are the sort of generally disesteemed, highly serious petty businessmen who have appeared in the earlier phases of economic revolution in many countries. Most of them belong to the same political and religious organizations; many of them are related either by blood or marriage; almost all of them have long been close acquaintances of one another. The individual innovator may operate more or less on his own in his economic activities, but in his effort to move from the traditional trader status to that of middle-class shopkeeper or small industrialist he is not alone, but forms part of a fairly solidary and rather self-conscious group. The processes of economic change in Modjokuto realize themselves, as they must, through individuals, but, as they have elsewhere, through individuals as members of social groups.

The fourth specific characteristic of Modjokuto's economic development is that it is both dependent upon and a response to a still incomplete revolution in the urban style of life (including that of urbanized elements in the villages) resultant upon the general transformations which have taken place in the town's social structure over the past decade or so. The most prominent of these transformations has been the emergence of the political parties, labor unions, women's clubs, youth societies, religious associations, and other mass organizations of the *aliran* pattern, the new bases of social ranking which have emerged with them, and the greatly expanded elementary and secondary school system which is inculcating the skills necessary to operate them. Together, these three institutional complexes have induced into the urban population the beginnings of a critical shift in taste. The notions of what is valuable and what is less so in the areas of consumption, of occupation, even of personal qualities are undergoing a steady change. It is the stucco bungalow, not the classic open-porch country house, which is coming to be the sign of elite status; it is the leader of the political party or of the labor union, rather than the civil servant, whose place is increasingly respected, envied, and striven for; it is educational attainment not fluency in traditional politesse which is increasingly looked up to as the most estimable sort of social skill. Particularly among the younger men, the so-called *pemuda* ("youth"), the models for living are being drawn from the Westernized, secularized culture of the

Djakarta and Surabaja seaport metropolises, rather than the classical court culture of such precolonial inland castle towns as Surakarta and Jogjakarta. It is in responding to this general shift in life style as it manifests itself in the economic field that the would-be entrepreneurial class has its main chance; for this shift makes possible both the sober, respected bourgeois role they seek and the sort of steadily broadening pattern of consumer tastes which can sustain it.

These four characteristics, then — a trading pattern foundation, the central importance of organizational problems in the innovational task, the rise of a socially well-demarcated entrepreneurial group, and a rapidly changing pattern of urban tastes — define the main co-ordinates of Modjokuto's developmental pattern and form the sociocultural space within which it is unfolding. But whether this unfolding will eventually complete itself or will prove abortive remains very much an open question. In general, two circumstances stand out as possibly, but not necessarily, forming insuperable obstacles to the achievement of genuine take-off in Modjokuto: one is the tremendous scale of the task involved in organizing the financing of modern, capital-intensive, heavy industry; the other is the presence of the Chinese.

Taking the second issue, the Chinese, first, it is clear that the relationship between them and the rising entrepreneurial class in the years immediately ahead will be an important determinative factor in the success of Modjokuto's development. In the race to become the town's modern middle class the Chinese have some tremendous advantages: they have more capital, more business acumen and experience, more organizational resources by far than the Javanese shopkeepers; but they have one tremendous disadvantage: they are Chinese. Resentment against them, always great, actually increases in direct proportion as they and their Javanese competitors gain in strength. In particular, the tension between the nascent entrepreneurial groups in the two communities (for the Chinese community has its traditionalists and its innovators also) intensifies as the stakes involved become increasingly clear. The Chinese are in the unenviable position of representing a "problem" which gets worse as Modjokuto develops, for the more that traditional status groups dissolve into heterogeneous social classes in the rest of the society, the more sharply the Chinese community stands apart as a separate, foreign entity, while at the same time the more its assimilation into that society seems to threaten the central interests of the embryonic and insecure Javanese business class So far, at least, it has proved much easier to throw out the Dutch than to take the Chinese in.

Since the Revolution (when there were a number of Javanese atrocities against Chinese in and around Modjokuto), governmental harassment of Chinese commerce has been persistently, if irregularly — and, so far as Modjokuto is concerned, more or less ineffectively — applied, and the traditional antagonism between Chinese and Javanese has been much accentuated. The fact that the most dynamic figures in the Modjokuto Chinese community are almost all China- rather than Indonesia-born and that many clearly owe their primary political loyalty to Peking has, of course, tremendously complicated the whole problem. In time, the emigration of young Chinese to China, which has greatly increased in the past few years, and the prohibition of immigration from China may serve to reduce the scope of the problem somewhat, but the vicious circle of suspicion, hatred, resentment, separateness, and reinforced suspicion on the part of the two communities promises to continue unabated for some years. On the one side the Javanese say the Chinese do not want to be Indonesians and on the other the Chinese say the Javanese will not allow them to be. And there is just enough truth in both accusations (and, of course, to a great extent such prejudices create the very reality which validates them) to make a rapprochement extremely difficult.

But short of a total solution through voluntary emigration, which seems rather unlikely, or some variant of Hitler's treatment of Germany's Jews, which would totally corrupt the moral foundations of Indonesian culture, such a rapprochement is ultimately inevitable: the culturally, ethnically, religiously, and socially insulated Chinese community is the town's outstanding relic of Modjokuto's prewar composite social structure, and until the "Chinese question" is answered the formation of a modern urban society in the town must remain but partially complete. Perhaps the greatest single contribution to the possibility of a just answer would be the disappearance in both the Javanese and Chinese business communities of the deeply ingrained bazaar economy premise that a Javanese cannot, in the very nature of the case, compete effectively with a Chinese in economic matters. So far as Modjokuto is concerned, that this is not so is demonstrated both by the role of the large Javanese traders up until the depression and by the activities of the more self-confident and successful Javanese shopkeepers and manufacturers of today. The determined struggle of the hat factory against its Chinese distributor, the hiring of a Chinese bookkeeper for the sugar factory, and the generally cordial relations between the Hadji storekeeper and his Chinese colleagues perhaps herald the emergence of a more hopeful pattern for the future — one in which Javanese inferiority and resentment and Chinese defensive arrogance will dissolve into feelings not of undying love but of mutual respect.

Thus, although the appearance of genuine entrepreneurs in both the Javanese and Chinese communities in Modjokuto may serve initially to intensify hostility between the two ethnic groups by bringing them into more direct opposition to one another, it may also contain the seeds of a resolution of that hostility and the establishment of more workable relations. Aided, perhaps, by a decrease in size of the Chinese community through emigration, by the expansion of opportunities in the economy, and by governmental legislation designed to stimulate the growth of small businesses in the population, Chinese-Javanese relations in Modjokuto may ultimately reach some sort of modern equilibrium. But whether the strains of development and the hostility such strains inevitably seem to generate will be outweighed by the decrease in inferiority feelings among the Javanese and in defensiveness among the Chinese is one of those moral imponderables which necessarily make social prediction inexact.[23]

The second circumstance which may form an important obstacle to the achievement of genuine take-off in Modjokuto is the

[23] The "Chinese problem" is, of course, much more than a purely economic one, and has a host of cultural, social, and psychological aspects. For a full description and analysis of the role of the Chinese in Modjokuto, see Edward Ryan, *The Chinese Community in Modjokuto* (in press).

so-called lumpiness problem. Recent economic theory, particularly of the linear programming sort, increasingly has come to emphasize the discontinuities in economic change, the quantum jumps which are often involved in moving from one set of production coefficients to another. Modern steel mills, automobile plants, and, for a case closer to the point, capital-intensive sugar refineries do not really come in all sizes, nor do they, nowadays, arise gradually by incremental changes from obscure beginnings; like Athena they are born adult. So, too, with whole economies there is some question as to whether a large-scale industrial structure can any longer rise directly out of a trade and small manufacturing pattern, or whether both extensive capital (and perhaps personnel) transfers and massive intervention by highly centralized government are not necessary. There arises the uneasy feeling that it is not the English but the Russian industrialization experience which is prototypical for our age, and that there is about Modjokuto's "shopkeeper revolution" an air of quaint irrelevancy.

Certainly, it is difficult to see the proprietor of Toko Kudus, for all his undoubted abilities, as coming to be the director of the Indonesian equivalent of Sears Roebuck; and there is no obvious way in which our small Javanese-sugar factory can evolve by minute gradations into a large modern refinery. Industrialization, in particular, will certainly demand large lumps of investment such as, in Indonesia, only government is going to be able to provide. The external economies large industries provide for one another demand that many of them (as well as various forms of social overhead capital) be constructed at the same time in a massive effort after "balanced growth"; and clearly such a massive effort is beyond the sort of petty capitalist entrepreneurial class we have described for Modjokuto any time in the foreseeable future. As examples of economic innovation, the activities of these men are perhaps of theoretical interest; but in practical, developmental terms, does what they are doing really matter?

It does, for several reasons. In the first place, without the growth of some sort of sturdy, indigenous, business class, the Indonesian government is likely to find the task of inducing rapid economic growth an insuperable one. Such a class provides the sort of human resources — in terms of skills, values, and motivations — without which industrial development is as impossible as it is without natural resources; and such resources cannot be created by fiat any more than can iron or coal deposits. Without some sort of internal impetus, independent of government action (and, after all, government personnel are also drawn from the general population, and so are likely to share its basic characteristics), it is doubtful indeed whether take-off can occur in Indonesia — or in any other country for that matter. It is one thing to stimulate, channel, and supplement the growth of a modern economy; it is quite another to create such an economy *ex nihilo* out of an almost wholly traditional culture. Whatever their shortcomings, Modjokuto's shopkeepers and manufacturers are what the Indonesian government has to work with.

Second, the concept of "balanced growth," whatever its uses on a normative level, is an overidealization of the process of economic development as it actually occurs, most particularly in the early phases. Multiple and unconnected regional expansion; intermittent and self-contained spurts of this industry or that; largely independent, even contradictory, institutional development are all characteristic of countries in pretake-off periods, and such inbalances may continue well beyond take-off.[24] It is not necessary that everything be done at once or that maximum integration be maintained at each and every stage of development. Indonesia may — looking at her geographical and cultural diversity, one is tempted to say necessarily will — develop in fits and starts rather than continuously, and in an uneven and disjointed rather than a systematic and co-ordinated manner. Whatever role a partial and circumscribed development such as Modjokuto's may come to play within the ultimate integration of a modernized Indonesian economy — and this of course depends to a great extent on how far similar developments are occurring elsewhere — it has a posi-

[24] As, for example, in Brazil or Turkey. Further, the view that Russian development consisted of a massive and historically almost instantaneous creation of a modern industrial structure whole and entire comes from the error of dating Russian growth from 1920 rather than from 1860. On the virtues of imbalanced growth generally, see A. O. Hirschman, *The Strategy of Economic Deveolypment* (New Haven, Conn.: Yale University Press, 1958).

tive significance in its own terms. In the sort of jammed and disorganized situation of Indonesia today, no genuine growing point is so small or so peripheral as to be irrelevant. And third, the problem of economic development cannot be wholly divorced from its political implications. Economic growth can occur under a variety of political forms and the admittedly outstanding achievements of a few recent totalitarian states in forcing rapid change ought not to blind us to the possibilities for equally outstanding achievements within frameworks less destructive of liberty and the meaningfulness of individual experience. In general, the contrast between government-directed great-leap-forward balanced growth and privately directed, step-by-step imbalanced growth has been much overdrawn, both in response to the ideological pressures of the cold war and as a result of the consistent tendency of social scientists to think entirely in terms of patterns which have already had a clear historical manifestation. But the possibility of economic revolution without extreme political rigidification in underdeveloped nations would seem to rest precisely on the possibility of avoiding a choice between an ineffectual, decentralized libertarianism and an efficient, managerial despotism. Although there is little doubt that government will have to play a leading role in economic planning in Indonesia, there is much more doubt that it will have to play a wholly dominant or simply self-sufficient one, and a productive interaction between large-scale state activities and less concentrated private ones is far from impossible. We have seen, in fact, how such an interaction actually took place, despite the tremendous obstacles created by the prejudices and inequalities of colonialism, in the prewar sugar boom. It seems likely that the future of the Indonesian economy lies neither wholly in Djakarta nor wholly in Modjokuto, but in the possibility of establishing a mutually stimulative relationship between them.

4. Economic Development in Tabanan

In Tabanan, the nascent entrepreneurial class of displaced aristrocrats is concerned not with reorganizing a bazaar economy but with readjusting an agrarian one. Rather than attempting to give some articulate form to an overfluid, individualistic trading pattern, they are trying to adapt the intensely collective and profoundly settled forms of traditional peasant society to the more various needs of a modern economy. Their task is one of loosening rather than tightening, of limbering rather than stiffening, for their aim is to apply long-solidified institutions to novel economic ends. By mobilizing habitual sentiments of loyalty, respect, obligation, and trust, they hope to make ancient custom serve modern enterprise. For the role of political princelet they wish to substitute that of economic lordling; or, as the leading young nobleman entrepreneur of the town said: "They've taken the government away from us — all right, we'll capture the economy!"

But, of course, the economy they wish to capture does not yet in fact exist. They must themselves create it. Like their Modjokuto counterparts, they must establish autonomous merchandising and manufacturing firms, institutional forms more or less novel to the society; the difference is that the social and cultural building blocks they have to use for this task come not from the bazaar but from the village. Enmeshed, as they have always been, in a

complex network of specific and explicit ties both with one another and with the great mass of commoners they once ruled, the
town-based aristocracy must manipulate these ties in such a way
as to construct enterprises which will be flexible in adjusting to
the rapid situational changes characteristic of a non-traditional
economy and yet rigid enough to permit persistent and systematic
activity. A successful Tabanan entrepreneur must face both for-
wards and backwards; he must combine in himself business acumen and cultural prestige; he must be able both to attract old
loyalties and to direct them to new purposes. For these reasons
a member of a tottering but still upright aristocracy is a logical
candidate for the role.

Progress toward more effective patterns of economic activity in
Tabanan consequently takes the form of a movement, hesitant
and circumscribed, from a peasant-village type economy toward
a firm-type economy. Development appears in the form of commercial and manufacturing enterprises held together by norms
derived from a primarily agrarian context. Of course, the contrast with Modjokuto is but one of emphasis — there, too, rural
values and classical patterns of prestige play a part, in the same
way as the bazaar pattern has not been wholly without effect in
Tabanan — but it is nevertheless real. In Tabanan, a modern
economy, so far as it is appearing at all, is arising more or less
directly out of the traditional gentry-peasantry pattern of social
relationships typical of so many of the great Asian civilizations,
and not out of a trading network inserted into this pattern under
the influence of foreign commerce. As such, an understanding of
this development demands a prior understanding of the organization of the Balinese village, particularly as it relates to economic
functions.

Rural Social Structure and Economic Organization[1]

The general organization of the Balinese village, and hence of its
economy — for the two cannot be sharply differentiated — is per-

[1] For a general description of Balinese village organization see C. Geertz,
"Form and Variation in Balinese Village Structure," *American Anthropologist*,
LXI (1959), 991–1012.

haps best seen as a set of the overlapping and intersecting corporate associations the Balinese call *seka* (literally: "to be as one";
"to be unified"). A *seka* is a social group, formed on the basis of
a single and exclusive criterion of membership, and dedicated to
a particular and usually rather narrowly specified social end, religious, political, economic, or whatever. Membership in some
seka is ascribed, in others it is more or less voluntary; some *seka*
are permanent and immortal institutions, some form and disband
with circumstances; some are central to the whole of Balinese
social organization, some are peripheral and secondary. In each
seka all members have absolutely equal rights and duties; no ex-
ternally based discriminations between their various roles are
acknowledged and no internally derived ones are permitted to
arise, although there are usually one or more hereditary or popularly chosen leaders, with diffuse and wholly non-authoritarian
directive and representative functions. Every Balinese belongs to
from three or four up to nearly a dozen of these groups, and the
value of *seka* loyalty, putting the needs of one's group above one's
own, is, along with caste pride, a central value in Balinese social
life.

This *seka* pattern of organization gives to Balinese village social
structure both a strongly collective and yet a peculiarly complex
and flexible pattern. Balinese do almost everything, even the
simplest of undertakings, in groups, in fact in groups which, as
Gregory Bateson and Margaret Mead have pointed out, almost
invariably involve personnel clearly far in excess of what is technically necessary.[2] The creation of a crowded, bustling, somewhat
disordered and hectic social environment — what the Balinese call
ramé, another primary value — seems to be requisite for the performance of even the most elementary tasks. And, as there sometimes seem to be almost as many differently composed groups as
there are tasks, the over-all structure is intricate indeed. This
combination of a somewhat antlike attack on the performance of
important social activities — which the Balinese themselves wryly
describe as *bebek-bebekan* ("duck-like"), after the way masses of

[2] G. Bateson and M. Mead, *Balinese Character* (New York: New York
Academy of Science, 1942).

happily quacking ducks waddle along the roads and canals in
tight formation — on the one hand, with a tendency to direct any
one group to a single end rather than employing the same group
for multiple purposes on the other, leads to what one might call,
paradoxically, a pluralistic collectivism. The cross-cutting of social
alliances means that almost no one is completely engrossed in
any single, totally comprehensive institution, without alternative
loyalties, to which he may have recourse against group pressures,
and yet no one is ever obliged to operate entirely on his own,
independently of some well-defined social aggregation. Balinese
society is not individualistic, but it is, nevertheless, rather libertarian in its own peculiar and traditionalist way. For all the
communalism, there is room for personal maneuver.

TYPES OF ECONOMIC GROUPING

In a rough and ready manner, the types of *seka* in Bali can
be divided into five main categories: (1) temple congregations,
(2) residential units, (3) irrigation and agricultural societies,
(4) kinship groups, and (5) voluntary associations. *Seka* of the first
type are, of course, primarily religious in their aims, those of
the second primarily political; but both have significant economic
implications and often perform specifically economic tasks. In
the last three the economic element stands out even more clearly.
In fact, almost the whole of Balinese economic life is realized
through one or another of these *seka*, strictly individual activity
being rather rare.

A Balinese temple congregation consists of a defined group of
people obligated both to worship at a given temple on certain
calendrical holy days and to maintain that temple in an order
fit for the divine attendance which takes place on these days. On
the one hand, this involves the organization and preparation of
elaborate ritual offerings of food, flowers, and cloth, which are
presented to the gods, as well as the numerous obeisances which
must be performed; on the other, it involves various financial
obligations connected with the upkeep of the temple. These last
are sometimes met by simple monetary assessments of the mem-

bers, or by working directly on the temple itself. Even more often, the charges are met by some sort of collective economic activity on the part of the congregation, the proceeds of which are then applied to the necessary repairs, paraphernalia, or whatever is necessary. Perhaps the most common practice is for the members of the congregation to harvest their several fields as a group in a "harvesting *seka*," and then to sell the traditional harvester's share (about one-tenth of the crop) on the open market to form a treasury for the temple. But other methods are also used. Rice-land may be bought in the temple's name, worked by members of the congregation in turn, and the proceeds from it used to increase the treasury. Talented congregations may give professional dance and dramatic performances to the same end. And congregations where there is some occupational specialty may work silver, manufacture musical instruments, or carve statues for the temple's benefit. Whether it be one of the traditional-origin, death, or fertility temples found in or near almost every Balinese settlement, a large state temple which a noble house "owns" but commoners support, a temple dedicated to some magical end, such as healing, or the commemoration of some mystical occurrence, such as an apparition, the rather highly ritualistic and very time-consuming Balinese ceremonial system provides both the motivation and the context for a wide range of quite secular economic activities.

The basic territorial community in Bali is the hamlet. A hamlet consists of anywhere from a dozen up to a couple of hundred households arranged in a nucleated settlement pattern and focused upon a communal meeting house. Monthly gatherings, held in this meeting house, are attended by one representative from each household, and all of the basic policy decisions for the hamlet as a whole are arrived at by means of open discussion in these gatherings, under the general leadership of popularly chosen hamlet officials. Since the hamlet usually owns the land on which the houseyards comprising it are built (and so regulates immigration), it can levy taxes, impose fines, and exile wrongdoers, and has the right to call upon its members for a wide range of public services — for example, constructing public buildings or repairing roadways — it is clearly the corporate unit of most general political significance on the local level.

But despite its primarily political emphasis, the hamlet, too, provides an important framework for economic activities. Here, also, the members may form a harvesting group to earn income for the treasury, and most hamlets own a public barn where the harvested rice may be stored until it is necessary to sell it. Hamlet-based dance groups, with the hamlet as a whole owning the *gamelan* orchestra and the costumes, and with the profits going into the hamlet treasury, are very common. And most hamlets own riceland — some a good deal — with one or another member of the hamlet working the land as a sharecropper, this job often being rotated among the landless of the hamlet as a welfare measure. In many hamlets members may even borrow up to a certain amount of money or rice from the hamlet treasury at a low interest rate for personal use.

In addition to these more traditional forms of economic co-operation, hamlets are engaging more and more in fairly modern types of business enterprise, setting up collectively owned coffee shops, retail stores, or even more complex organizations such as brick or tile factories. Two examples of this sort of activity, one involving a bus line, the other a successful producer's and con-summer's co-operative, may be offered for illustrative purposes.

The assembly of one isolated mountain hamlet some fifteen kilometers or so northwest of Tabanan came to the conclusion that the community lacked two items which had become of alto-gether crucial importance in post-Revolutionary "modern" Bali: good transportation facilities to the town of Tabanan, and an elementary school. The town-based bus companies judged the hamlet too far off the beaten track to be worth extending service to, and the government naturally favored spending its limited resources for school construction in areas where a larger popula-tion could be served. The hamlet members decided to sell off the hamlet riceland and various other communal properties and to assess themselves a certain, rather stiff amount in order to buy a secondhand bus to belong to the hamlet as a corporation. One of the landless members was given a salaried job as chauffeur and mechanic, and a daily round-trip run to Tabanan was instituted. The bus-line profits, which turned out to be fairly good, were then applied to the building of the desired school and to the paying of teachers. Actually, the pay of the two teachers — both normal-school-educated outsiders — is still irregular, being dependent upon how the bus traffic is running, but some of the better-off members of the community provide room and board for them for almost nothing, so the project has been successful for over two years. Here, the political community of the hamlet has been made to form the basis of an autonomous business enterprise, the success of the venture clearly resting upon the strong feelings of solidarity and mutual trust engendered by hamlet living.

An even more striking example of this sort of collective rural entrepreneurship is offered by one of Bali's most successful co-operatives in Blaju, a village area about fifteen kilometers northeast of Tabanan town. In general, Balinese co-operatives have not tended to do well, in great part because they very early became deeply involved in political party factionalism, but also because they demand modern types of accounting and administrative skill not commonly found in the villages. But that in Blaju — where all the inhabitants belong to a single political party — has been extremely successful. Today the co-operative is supported, not by one but by the entire population of some sixteen neighboring hamlets, giving it a total membership of over seven hundred household heads. Each member must contribute one coconut and two kilograms of (unthreshed) rice a month; and in four years the capital of the enterprise has grown from Rp. 16,000 to Rp. 119,000, the permanent staff from two to eleven, and the range of activities has widened to include petty manufacturing as well as commerce.

The main activity of the co-operative lies in rice trading. With storage facilities for sixteen metric tons built on rent-free hamlet land, it buys about fifty tons a year, disposing of it both to its own members and, through the agency of the government co-operative bureau, to civil-servant consumer co-operatives in the large towns of Den Pasar and Singaradja. Further, about 70 per cent of this rice is bought whole and processed by the co-operative, which puts it out to local women who thresh and mill it, basket by basket, in their homes. All transactions are in cash, and both pick-up and delivery are by co-operative-owned trucks. Dry season crops — mainly soya beans in this area — are also bought and sold to Den Pasar Chinese, but, unlike Modjokuto, dry crop trading is still not of great importance in this area. In addition to crop trading the co-operative runs a retail store, in which are sold the usual small hardware, home furnishings, patent medicines, soft drinks, cigarettes, Javanese sugar, ready-made garments, kerosene, and so on. Also it operates a copra oven, manufactures roof tiles on a jobbing basis, exports pigs, and manages a small savings and loan bank for members. Obviously, this enterprise, based on and growing out of traditional hamlet ties, has begun to approach independent, firmlike status. Yet it remains a quasi-political, diffusely social institution, for the sanctions which maintain it are not differentiated from the general sanctions of hamlet life, and its continued viability depends very directly upon the broader processes of the particular hamlet social organizations which support it. It is, in a useful distinction recently proposed by Polanyi, Arensberg, and Pearson, an economic institution almost wholly "embedded" in customary, *seka*-type social structure, not an "unembedded" autonomous business enterprise.[3]

Aside from traditional collective effort patterns and semi-modern enterprises based on ascribed territorial ties, a third way in which the political structure of the hamlet intersects with economic concerns is in the matter of "village specialization." Unlike Java, where village-based industry is now of only marginal importance, Bali has maintained a strong tradition of rural handicraft, and these handicrafts show a marked tendency to be associated with particular hamlets in particular areas. In one hamlet almost everyone makes tiles, in the next nearly everyone manufactures musical instruments, or works silver, or manufactures salt, or weaves, or makes pots, or produces coconut oil. All the carpenters in a locality hail from one place, all the tailors from another, all the palm-wine makers from a third, and so on.

[3] K. Polanyi, C. M. Arensberg and H. W. Pearson, *Trade and Markets in the Early Empires* (Glencoe, Ill.: Free Press, 1957).

Only a minority of Balinese hamlets are thus specialized, of course; most are typically undifferentiated, rice-growing societies. But those which are specialized — and the tendency extends to the subhamlets of a town such as Tabanan — tend to merge hamlet political organization and economic specialty into a kind of guild structure, often with traditionally fixed relationship to clients in other hamlets, customary standards of quality, specific patterns of co-operation and competition, and so on. "Village specialization" imbeds economic activities even more deeply into the *seka*-structure and fuses general social membership and occupation even more intimately.

But one altogether crucial economic activity, which in Java and much of the rest of monsoon Asia is directly imbedded in village political structure, here lies outside the purview of the hamlet altogether: wet-rice agriculture. In Bali, field-crop cultivation is carried on within the general framework of a separate and independent *seka*-type organization specifically devoted to it and usually referred to in English as an "irrigation society," although "agricultural association" would be a more accurate term as water control represents only one of its functions.

The members of an irrigation society consist of all those individuals who own riceland which is irrigated from a single watercourse — a single dam and canal running from dam to fields. Since Balinese land ownership is very fragmented, a man's holdings typically consisting of one or two quarter-acre plots scattered about the countryside, often at some distance from his home, the members of one irrigation society almost never hail from a single hamlet, but from ten or fifteen different ones, while from the point of view of the individual hamlet, its members will commonly own land in a large number of irrigation societies, a smaller or greater distance away. The irrigation society is thus a completely specialized and autonomous corporate social organization, its membership coinciding wholly with that of no other social organization in the society, and as such it is perhaps the prime example of Bali's pluralistic collectivism — the tendency to attack problems co-operatively while distributing group loyalties segmentally.

The main functions of the irrigation society are the management of water resources, the co-ordination of planting, and the performance of agricultural rituals. Headed by a chief, usually popularly chosen, the irrigation society builds and maintains its dams and canals, and determines, in concert, the distribution of water among the individual fields. It also decides when planting shall take place and, for dry season crops, sometimes even what shall be planted. And, finally, it usually maintains two temples, one dedicated to the goddess of fertility, the other to the god of water, where members perform periodic ceremonies. The actual details of operation of the irrigation society, levying fines and assessments, constructing hundreds of small bamboo water-dividers to direct the flow of water, the exact arrangement of often fairly intricate crop rotation schemes, collecting taxes, and keeping land records, are extremely complex. The main point in this context is that almost every male adult Balinese has had, through one or more irrigation societies, the experience of working in a well-organized group devoted to purely economic ends of a rather specific, almost technical sort. True, the pattern is highly traditional — we hear of irrigation societies as early as the eleventh century[4] — but nevertheless it offers perhaps the closest approximation to a differentiated business firm, the best paradigm of a modern economic enterprise, found in classical village society.

In fact, with the recent growth in population, as well as increasing urbanization, there has arisen, especially in the larger irrigation societies, a tendency for even greater differentiation and specialization, a tendency best exemplified by the appearance of the so-called water-*seka*. A water-*seka* consists of a certain percentage of the total irrigation society membership, usually the less well-to-do individuals, who take on the entire responsibility for keeping the dams in repair and the canals clean — a task involving almost continual labor — in return for a monetary payment from individual members of the society, fixed according to the amount of land each owns. In a few societies, even four or five landless

[4] See J. L. Schwelengrabel, "An Introduction to Bali" in *Bali, Studies in Life, Thought and Ritual* (The Hague and Bandung: W. Van Hoeve, 1960).

non-members of the society are permitted to belong to the water-*seka*, thus in effect hiring themselves out as agricultural laborers, a practice otherwise uncommon in Bali. The water-*seka* — which functions only in irrigation matters as such — represents, therefore, the emergence of a specialized work-crew hired by the society as a whole to replace the egalitarian mutual co-operation of the traditional irrigation group, where calculation of individual contributions and returns was both less careful and less conscious. The final stage of this process is perhaps represented by the (admittedly still unusual) formation under energetic rural entrepreneurs, of wholly professional water-*sekas*, composed almost entirely of landless villages who belong to no irrigation society at all, and which hire out, on a jobbing basis, to perform the water management tasks for three or four different irrigation societies, certainly a very close approximation to a non-traditional unimbedded economic enterprise. For the most part, however, the irrigation society remains a typical Balinese *seka*: a group of mutually concerned individuals operating in a broadly collective way to perform a general social task, in this case food production.[5]

The relationship between *seka*-organization in the field of kinship, our fourth category, and economic activity is rather more difficult to describe because it varies so widely with circumstance and because a genuine understanding of Balinese kinship organization and its role in rural society demands a rather extended and detailed technical analysis. For our purposes here it is perhaps enough to say that the Balinese reckon descent patrilineally, that they live in extended family compounds containing from one up to nearly a dozen elementary families — though two or three families to a compound is the most common, and many families live alone — and that they are partially organized into large, semi-endogamous corporate kin groups which, in some hamlets but not in others, play an important role in village life. And for an example of how this sort of structure, when full-blown, may form the framework for economic enterprise, we may look briefly at

---

[5] The actual cultivation of the fields is accomplished individually, through exchange labor patterns, or by *seka* especially formed for the purpose — planting *seka*, weeding *seka*, etc.

the organization of the musical-instrument-making craft in Tihingan, Klungkung.[6]

Musical-instrument making in Bali is a smithing craft, because the instruments consist of bronze metallophones, cymbals, and gongs of various shapes and sizes which, mounted on wooden stands and supplemented by drums, make up the famous *gamelan* orchestras of the island. Tihingan is the only hamlet on Bali which still specializes in the manufacture and repair of these instruments, and although it is possible that the craft was in ancient times a monopoly of the smith, or Pandé, caste, today members of all lower-cast groups in Tihingan engage in it. Altogether, a total of some 53 per cent of the 171 adult males living in the hamlet draw a significant part of their income from this work, and among these there are five master craftsmen, thirty-five ordinary craftsmen, and forty-eight common laborers. With four large forges where the huge gongs are made and twenty-one small forges where the ordinary pieces are turned out, the almost constant clang of metal-pounding is the characteristic sound of the hamlet, the weary, soot-blackened smith the most characteristic sight.

The kinship organization of this craft is clear and explicit. There are essentially two types of work involved: the molding, shaping, and finishing of dozens of small metallophone keys, cymbals, and kettledrum-like instruments called *trompong*; and the pounding of the very large gongs. The first sort of activity takes place in the small forges and is performed piecemeal but at a more or less steady pace by from three to six men working together. The metal is first melted down in the forge by the use of a piston bellows, then poured into an earthen mold set in the ground, cooled, hammered into shape by alternate heating and anvil-pounding, and then finally finished and tuned by various techniques of filing and polishing, the whole process usually tak-

---

[6] A similar analysis could have been presented for a weaving hamlet near Tabanan and would perhaps have been more directly relevant to Tabanan town's development as such. But as the author lived for six months in Tihingan, his information on the instrument-makers is much more detailed and reliable, and the differences between Klungkung — in southeastern Bali — and Tabanan — in southwestern — are only minor.

Ing several weeks to complete. The second type of activity is performed in one all-out effort by fifteen to twenty men working at fever pitch. After the melting and molding the pounding takes a full day of constant work, and then the gong, which does not have to be filed and polished, is finished. Six men stand in a half-circle around the anvil and pound the gong steadily in rapid succession as it is turned by a seventh man, and, every two or three minutes, tempered by an eighth. This procedure goes on without a moment's pause from daybreak until dusk, the various workers spelling one another as they tire. Both the modes of work and the amount of labor demanded thus differ fairly radically between the two sorts of effort: in the first, small-scale, steadily proceeding, humdrum endeavor, which makes up the bulk of the work, the males of the patrilineal extended family, whether living in one courtyard or several, compose the work group; in the second, large-scale, all-at-once, more dramatic effort, the whole kin-group is mobilized.

When a craftsman secures a contract either for a whole *gamelan* or, more commonly, to replace a few worn-out instruments within an existing *gamelan*, he calls always upon his most immediate patri-kinsmen, and, without question, they set to work manufacturing the smaller pieces.[7] With very rare exceptions, unrelated individuals never work together in these groups, nor does a more distant relative participate when a closer one is available; a

[7] Market relationships are, in general, as highly traditional as are methods of work. Certain smith families make and repair *gamelans* for certain hamlets, others for others, and these relationships are enduring, passing from father to son (the fact that each smith family tunes its instruments slightly differently supports this whole process). The smith is often at least partially paid in kind (land, rice, etc.), or return services (such as housebuilding) and sometimes occupies a special ritual role in the hamet for which he makes the orchestra — e.g., he is obliged to attend the main temple ceremonies in which it is used. The above sketch of instrument-making as a traditional craft is very much schematized and sharply focused on the particular problem at hand, the kinship organization of production, because a full analysis would take us too far into Balinese technics (both musical and metalworking), Balinese history, Balinese social organization, and Balinese culture. For some general notes on the semimagical role of smiths and smithing in Bali see R. Goris, *De Positie der Pande Wesi* (Singaradja, Indonesia: Mededeelingen v/d Kirtya Liefrinck-van der Tuuk, Aflevering 1, 1929), pp. 44–49.

careful plotting of the location of forges and the men who work in them shows an almost exact fit with the distribution of extended family clusters within the hamlet. The workers are paid according to their skill, the exact division differing somewhat from group to group and from job to job. The initiator of the work does not necessarily own the forge — though he must be a competent craftsman — because within these small, tightly knit kin-units, equipment, though technically owned individually, is communally used, and a man aways has the right to claim the forge of his patri-cousin, father's brother, etc., as well as his labor. Thus, though the composition of this elemental work group stays fairly constant, organizational leadership shifts easily among the full craftsmen who belong to it. The whole procedure is definitely group-centered, and the workers are, inevitably, referred to not as a family, which is what they really are, but as a *seka*.

The making of the large gongs, on the other hand, can only take place under the direction of an experienced master craftsman — for the technical requirements involved are much more exacting and errors in judgment much more serious — and in a much larger forge. Usually almost all instrument-makers in a kin-group are invited to participate in such a job and are again morally obliged to do so. The initiator usually supplies an elaborate midday meal over and above the monetary payments involved, so that the making of a large gong, which will take place only every month or two in the best of times, takes on, for all the backbreaking labor involved, the air of a family festival. But, because of the heavy labor requirements, it is only the larger kin-groups who can engage in this activity in the first place. In Tihingan, only the three largest of the twelve kin groups in the hamlet, containing forty-seven, twenty-six, and twenty-five households respectively, possess large forges and count master craftsmen among their members, the other forty households having only a few ordinary craftsmen and a few fitfully operated small forges for minor repair work.[8] It is the mobilization of an extensive kin-group for co-

---

[8] Eighty-eight per cent of the skilled instrument-workers (i.e., master and ordinary craftsmen) and 84 per cent of the forges belong to the three largest kin-groups, which comprise only 68 per cent of the population.

operative endeavor which makes the very lucrative production of the large gongs possible, and as this mobilization further strengthens kin ties the relationship is a mutually reinforcing one. Again, although only a master craftsman has the necessary skills to direct large gong-making effectively, any ordinary craftsman in the kingroup *seka* may contract such a job and organize such a work party, "borrowing" (with appropriate recompense, of course) both the master craftsman and his forge for the purpose, and calling on kinsmen for the necessary skilled and unskilled labor, so that, once more, the work is clearly group-oriented and the *seka* ideal of a massive attack on a common task the controlling norm.

This collective, yet specialized, approach to economic activities, and in fact to entrepreneurship and innovation as such, is demonstrated clearly when one looks at the historical development in Tihingan of the making of large gongs, which is actually quite recent. There is a general tradition that large gongs were manufactured in the hamlet during precolonial times, but during the late nineteenth and early twentieth centuries they certainly were not. Tihingan craftsmen turned out only the small metallophones, cymbals, and gongs, and larger gongs — which they felt were beyond their technical capacities — had to be imported from Java. During the Japanese occupation, however, such importing became impossible, and pressured by the unsatisfied market (as well as by a progressive shift in Balinese musical tastes toward large, noisier, and less subtle orchestras) the Tihingan craftsmen slowly began to make bigger and bigger gongs. The process of change was gradual, pragmatic, collective, and competitive. When an individual secured a contract for a slightly larger gong than any his small extended family *seka* had ever made, he would call together a somewhat more extensive group of kinsmen and ask them if they were prepared to attempt this more formidable and risky task. If they were, and if they were successful, then the other local kin-groups would be envious and feel that their pride had been severely damaged, for rivalry among the main kin-groups is, and always has been, very intense; the sound of another group's hammers is galling to any Tihingan craftsman, best drowned by pounding one's own hammers the harder. The other groups would thus be goaded into attempting a gong of equal or slightly larger size, the first would respond, and so on, until after a few years everyone was making gongs about as large as is practical from a musical standpoint. In this experimental period, many mistakes were made, many costly and pride-injuring failures experienced — for the technical requirements of large gong-making differ notably from those involved in the smaller pieces — but slowly skill was, in a practical and almost unconscious manner, gained: "No one taught us," the craftsmen say today, "the work taught us." Here is an example of true group entrepreneurship, for even now no one can pick out individuals who persistently and clearly took the lead in this major innovation in a traditional craft; contracts for large gongs were secured by a wide range of persons, and each kin-group, in competition with its rivals, did its pioneering together, though as time passed certain more skilful individuals emerged as the group's master craftsmen.[9] Thus, social structures of even the most highly traditional sort are not inevitably barriers to change but can and do stimulate and support economic innovation, given a suitable pattern of pressures and opportunities.

The final sort of *seka*, purely voluntary ones, are more numerous, more variegated, and more purely economic (though there are non-economic voluntary *seka* — poetry-reading groups or religious societies, for example — as well). In almost every hamlet one finds three or four of these ten- to twenty-man groups dedicated to building up a treasury, to be divided equally among them, or to be used for a feast at *Galungan*, the major calendrical holiday. Agricultural *seka* which plant, weed, harvest and carry sheaves from the fields for a share in kind are very common. Other *seka* pick coconuts and hunt coconut squirrels for their livelihood. Others make house roofing from various grasses and palms, build and operate small Ferris wheels for holiday celebrations, or trans-

[9] The lines between laborers, craftsmen, and master craftsmen are not, in any case, clearly drawn and have no other ritual or other institutional symbolic support. A master craftsman is merely a man who, everyone knows, has a competence superior enough to that of his fellows to lead a large-gong party effectively. Further, the roles of master craftsman and craftsman have little or no importance outside the immediate gong-making task, either in the kin-group or in hamlet society as a whole. All these roles are specifically occupational and based on a quite informal consensus.

port goods to and from the town market. Dance, drama, and music groups perform publicly for hamlets, kin-groups, temple congregations, or individuals who hire them, the best ones traveling continually all over the islands. Local hawkers of iced drinks, sweets, or cooked rice band together to hold cockfights to stimulate their businesses (they take a cut on the betting too, which as they are risking arrest, is not unreasonable). Tile-making, pot-making, house-building, and other handicrafts are often organized on a voluntary *seka* basis, the main tie between the members aside from the technical one being that of friendship and mutual trust.

Sometimes several of these tasks are performed by a single, well-established and long-persisting *seka*, which thus takes on definitely firmlike attributes. For example, in the above mentioned hamlet of Tihingan, twenty men, from varying kin-groups, sections of the hamlet, and caste groups, are organized into a "workers' *seka*." Their major task is caring for the coconut trees belonging to the hamlet under a sharecropping arrangement in which they get one-third of the coconuts, the hamlet two-thirds. But they also perform various agricultural tasks for private parties — planting, harvesting, and so on — as well as whatever other manual labor opportunity offers, such as the building of a small shed to house a coffee shop. The *seka*, which has persisted ten years and has amassed a treasury of over 2,000 rupiah, also owns a third share in a large 600-rupiah handcart (the other two shares are held by the hamlet and by the town's richest extended family), which is rented out to individuals both within the hamlet and from other hamlets, who need it to cart bricks and market goods, the workers' *seka* sometimes providing the labor involved as well.

An even more advanced voluntary *seka* of this sort is found in a hamlet a few kilometers outside Tabanan. This *seka*, which also consists of twenty individuals — most of them fairly solid hamlet citizens, performs all sorts of work. It plants, weeds, and harvests; it builds houses — for the leading figures in it are carpenters and bricklayers; it prepares and sells copra; and, manufacturing its own tools, it saws wood into lumber at one cent a metric foot. In a period of five years, this *seka* has accumulated more than Rp. 3,500. It has also taken several pieces of rice land in pawn, and has lent money to various of its members to get their land out of pawn, the loans being gradually paid back in terms of half the yearly harvest of the fields involved.[10] Finally, the *seka* has even gone so far as to invest Rp. 1,000, at 2 per cent interest, in a small, new hardware store in Tabanan town, owned by a hamlet-dwelling entrepreneur. Clearly, this *seka* is a going business concern, conducted along rational lines, although the diffuse friendship ties that bind it together are traditional, personal ones.

It is to be emphasized again that these sorts of *seka* are not atypical in the Balinese rural scene; one finds something like them in almost every hamlet. Nor are they, so far as we can see, wholly new developments, but are a deeply rooted type of institution in Balinese society. *Seka* organization, whether religious, political, agricultural, kinship, or voluntarily based, is the heart of Balinese social structure, which can, in fact, be seen as a set of cross-cutting *seka* of various types loosely adjusted to one another. And it is on the basis of this type of pluralistic collectivism — in such marked contrast to the hyperindividuated, person-to-person bazaar pattern with which Modjokuto's would-be firm-builders must cope — that the aristocratic entrepreneurs of Tabanan town must base their efforts after innovation, reform, and economic growth.

The Tabanan Aristocracy[11] *and the Firm-Type Economy*

One of the most persistent, most widespread, and most fallacious scholarly stereotypes of Indonesian social organization — as in-

[10] When a man pawns his land, the man who takes it in pawn has full use of it until the pawn is redeemed; the fertility of the field acts as interest on the loan. Most pawns are without terms, and land in pawn may descend for generations with the original owner's descendants always reserving the right to pay off the pawn and take back the land.

[11] In the sequel the terms "aristocrat" and "noble," together with their various cognates, are used interchangeably to mean "member of the patrilineally defined traditional royal family of Tabanan," irrespective of actual closeness to the living king, which in Bali determines the relative status of "aristocrats" or "nobles." A more fine-grained political analysis would make

correct for Java as it is for Bali — is that it consists, and has for
centuries consisted, of almost wholly independent, closed-in,
peasant communities, socially insulated, self-absorbed "village
republics" (to use a favorite and wholly misleading term popular
among Dutch writers) enduring, passively and patiently, beneath
an equally self-contained and aloof, though much more unstable,
gentry ruling class. "The feudalism of the Hindu [sic] aristocracy
was curiously only superimposed on the Balinese patriarchal communism, and centuries of feudal rule have failed to do away with
the closed independence of the village communities," writes
Covarrubias, in what is otherwise probably the most useful popular survey of Balinese culture in English; [12] and through almost
all the writings on prewar Bali this same theme runs: kings,
dynasties, whole ruling classes come and go, but the unconcerned
peasant, the "real, original Balinese," for whom such political
upheavals merely signify a change of tax collector, plods on forever in the unchanging paths of uncounted centuries. Between
noble and commoner, relations are conceived to have always been
ones of pure hostility and a direct opposition of interests, and the
present integrity of rural society is taken as a simple measure of
the degree to which the villager has been able to set his face
against the wholly destructive encroachments of his self-appointed
rulers:

> The primitive Balinese socialism flourished parallel to
> medieval feudalism despite five centuries of domination by
> an aristocracy that with all its ruthlessness could not break
> down the inherent unity and cooperativism of the Balinese
> communities. The nobility met with insurmountable passive
> resistance to any encroachments upon the autonomy of the
> villages and had finally to content themselves with the collec-
> tion of tribute from their "vassals." The common people
> tolerated the princes, but even today they consider them as
> total outsiders and in most social and administrative matters
> the villages remain entrenched against all interference from

more careful distinctions, but for our purposes the gross opposition of aristocrat to commoner (including, in this case, non-noble upper-caste individuals)
will suffice.

[12] M. Covarrubias, *Island of Bali* (New York: Knof, 1937), p. 57.

the noble landlords, now appointed as go-betweens between the people and the Dutch Government. . . .[13]

This view of gentry-peasantry relationships — a reflex both of colonial ideologies justifying Western rule as freeing the mass of the population from medieval tyranny, and of anthropological romanticism glorifying the "simple villager" as representing the essence of Asian culture, rather than a conclusion from a systematic analysis of the organization of the indigenous Balinese state — is thoroughly misconceived. The Balinese gentry were not "outsiders," but, from the very beginning, an integral part of Balinese society.[14] They were not simply tribute-takers, but performed altogether crucial, interlocal, political, religious, and economic functions upon which the supposedly self-subsisting village was dependent for its very existence. And, far from having no essential effect on rural social structure, they were one of the primary forces determining its ultimate shape. Although the caste barrier between aristocrat and commoner was indeed almost impermeable, the etiquette of deference extraordinarily well developed, and the lines between local and supralocal concerns very sharply drawn, the two groups played complementary rather than contradictory roles in traditional Balinese society, and both the Balinese state and the Balinese village became what they became in great part as a result of the close, multifaceted, long-term, and ever changing interaction they had with one another. "Primitive Balinese socialism" — the *seka* system — represented not a bulwark against "medieval feudalism" — traditional state organization — but an integral part of it.

For our purposes, it is unnecessary to describe this interdependency between village and state in detail. What is of impor-

[13] *Ibid.*, p. 400.
[14] The importance of the actual migration of Javanese aristocrats to Bali after the fall of Madjapahit, and the Islamization of Java in the fifteenth century, in the formation of upper-caste Balinese culture has been much overestimated in writings on the history of Bali. The growth of the Balinese gentry appears to have been largely endogenous. For the great number of inscriptions indicating the existence of pre-Madjapahit culture on Bali, see R. Goris, *Prasasti Bali* (Singaradja, Indonesia: Mededeelingen v/d Kirtya Liefrinck-van der Tuuk, Aflevering 1, 1958).

tance is to stress that the ruling groups, themselves organized mainly into various royal and noble lines, were not simply "outside" and "above" the sort of social organization we have described for the villages, but maintained direct and important links with it. Political, military, ceremonial, economic, kinship, and other ties all bound aristocrat and commoner together into a single structure. And it was these ties — and the loyalties which they created and maintained — which formed the foundation for aristocratic leadership in all matters on a supravillage, translocale scale, a leadership which Tabanan's upper-caste entrepreneurs are attempting to continue in the economic realm today.

The politico-military ties between lord and commoner have already been briefly described: deliberately cross-cutting rural social groupings, these personalistically phrased loyalties were used to mobilize the population as a self-armed militia as occasion demanded, for professional standing armies did not exist in traditional Bali. With the sound of the hamlet slit-gong the able-bodied men of the neighborhood rushed forth with kris, spear, and packet of rice to join the war camp — the military *seka* — of one or another lord.[15] Legal issues which transcended hamlet lines, either geographically or in their very nature (e.g., miscaste marriages) were judged and punished in lords' courts; the riceland and other property (including, often, their wives) of men dying without direct patrilineal heirs fell to the control of their lords; the execution of serious hamlet-passed criminal sentences were often left to the lords, and so on. Exiles from the hamlets out of poverty, restlessness, or a chronic inability to conform clustered

[15] In some areas, including Tabanan, all adult men were so obligated to fight, in others only a percentage who worked communal riceland were liable, and in all areas there were various gradations and types of service. The problem of military organization was, of course, enormously complicated by the fact that extended campaigns — which were rare — raised crucial logistic problems, and that alliances among lords, even with single family lines, shifted rather easily. It is also true — though the point has been much overstressed in the literature — that there were differences in the degree of influence of lords in village affairs according to the closeness of the hamlet to the lord's seat, so that obscure mountain villages could often maintain fairly high levels of autonomy and independence of upper-caste interference. A full analysis of Balinese state organization, covering in detail the various aspects mentioned in passing here, will be undertaken in a forthcoming monograph.

around the noble palaces as fully dependent retainers, and in the hamlets themselves certain eminent families were designated the official representatives of this lord or that — a link commonly solidified by the giving of a wife or two to the lord's harem — and were privileged to exercise his authority and display his prestige there. Thus, each lord formed for the village people the center of a quite explicitly defined network of political-jural obligations, rivaling in importance those to temple, hamlet, irrigation society, kin-group, or voluntary association.

In the symbolic, broadly cultural, religious and artistic spheres, the upper castes were of no less importance as mobilizers, generalizers, and integrators. In the first place, the massive religious ceremonials they conducted in their palaces — tooth-filings, cremations, temple consecrations — not only mobilized their subjects into large-scale corvée-like co-operative endeavor for their realization, but also depended upon them for material contributions and for an audience. The great collective ritual dramas, which reached spectacular levels of display, probably did as much or more toward shaping and intensifying ties between lord and subject as did politico-military adventures: in a royal or noble *karja* — literally, a "work" — the Balinese saw summed up many of the essentials of his culture; the lord expressed in his near-divine status, in his ostentation, in his whole Hinduized style of life, the grandeur which the Balinese social system could, when properly organized and directed, attain.

In the second place, the lord's role as art patron linked him to village aesthetic life, in many ways the core of its existence. Some of the finest *gamelan* orchestras were owned by lords and lent to village *seka* to play. Court dancing was the model for the finest village dancing, and many of the most talented young boys and girls of the countryside went to live at the court as servants in order to study with the great teachers there, some of whom were themselves but talented commoners. And most of the fine commoner craftwork groups — the silversmiths, the woodcarvers, the instrument-makers — had traditionally established ties of a special sort with one or another of the courts. And, third, the high-caste Brahmana priest, formulator and perpetuator of the systematized, Hindu aspect of Balinese religion, and identified in both fact and theory with the ruling families, played an important role in village ritual life, for it was only from him that the holy water necessary for the most crucial ceremonies could be obtained.[16] The view of Robert Redfield that "peasant culture" displays a constant interchange between the reflective, systematized "great tradition" of the gentry and the concrete, ritualistic "little tradition" of the peasantry is clearly demonstrated in Balinese history, and what Marriot has written of the Indian village of Kishan Gari holds as well for the Balinese villages:

> Seen through its festivals and deities, the religion of the village . . . may be conceived as resulting from continuous processes of communication between a little, local tradition and greater traditions which have their places partly inside and partly outside the village [so that] only residual fragments of the religion of such a little community can be conceived as distinctive or separable.[17]

Finally, of course, there were important gentry-peasantry ties of a more or less purely economic nature. We have already briefly discussed sharecropping relations between lord and tenant, and pointed out how these increased in importance after political corvée was abolished by the Dutch. Before this period the tenant's obligations to his landlord, qua tenant, consisted almost wholly of his rent, varying from one half to three-quarters of the harvest, depending upon local custom. Yet the large-scale holdings of the nobles, accumulated by war, by the attachment of land lacking direct heirs or whose owner had committed a felony, and sometimes even by purchase from other nobles, meant that the eco-

[16] Each Brahmana priest "owns" from a half-dozen up to hundreds of non-Brahmana "students" who are traditionally obliged to come to him exclusively for their holy water and for various other ritual needs. The students of any one priest, who is referred to as their "teacher," are not located in any single village, but are scattered through many villages, four here, five there, and so on, which yields a pattern similar to that of lords and subjects described above.

[17] McKim Marriot, "Little Communities in an Indigenous Civilization," in McKim Marriot (ed.), *Village India* (Chicago: University of Chicago Press, 1955), pp. 171–222. For Redfield's views, see R. Redfield, *Peasant Society and Culture* (Chicago: University of Chicago Press, 1956).

nomic life of much of the peasantry was directly intertwined with that of the gentry. In irrigation, too, the lords played an important role in co-ordinating activities between irrigation societies and settling interlocal disputes, granting rights to clear new land, build new dams, and form new societies, and so on. Usually a member of the royal house was appointed general overseer of irrigation for the whole region, and each noble house had one or two irrigation officials of its own. The role of the state in irrigation matters can easily be much exaggerated – as it has been, for Bali at least, in Wittfogel's recent treatment of "Oriental Despotism" – for in essence the irrigation societies were self-directing associations of those directly involved and not mere appendages of a central bureaucracy, but it is clear that upper-caste "interference" in local agricultural matters was not restricted wholly to the extortion of "tribute" but fulfilled an important and sometimes innovative function.[18] In the area of trade, not only did the nobility tend to control the crafts and monopolize foreign commerce through contracts with Chinese, as already explained, but most of the important local markets, sheltered against the wall of a palace, seem to have been gentry owned, managed, and, of course, taxed. As in politics, religion, and art, so in economics the rulers and the ruled represented not parallel but completely intersecting social groups.

It is this heritage of indisputable leadership in supralocal affairs which the Tabanan aristocracy is now attempting to turn to their account in building an urban-based, nationally oriented firm economy. In contrast to the Modjokuto small businessmen, whose puristic Islamic piety represents a nonconformist, variant, even somewhat denigrated, pattern within the local culture, the Tabanan entrepreneurs, or the great majority of them in any case, are cultural exemplars – they symbolize the quintessence of indigenous culture, demonstrate its furthest reaches of complexity, refinement, and sophistication. Though their treatment (or, more

[18] K. Wittfogel, *Oriental Despotism* (New Haven, Conn.: Yale University Press, 1957). The relationship between irrigated agriculture and political authoritarianism in Bali needs much more study before Wittfogel's generalizations about "hydraulic society" can be deemed applicable.

exactly that of their forefathers) of commoners was indeed often intensely oppressive, not to say brutal, and the sentiments directed toward them by the villagers in turn were probably more of awe than affection, the nobility, supplemented by the priesthood, has always appeared to almost the entire population as the proper vehicle of Bali's claim to be a true world civilization rather than an isolated, neolithic backwater. And today, when many of the specific structural arrangements which supported this role of cultural representative have been either dissolved or drastically reorganized, the sentiments which underlie them persist. In their bid to "capture the [modern] economy" the aristocrats have at their disposal a quantity of cultural capital in the form of traditional social loyalties and expectations which Modjokuto's self-made shopkeepers entirely lack.

SOME MODERN ENTERPRISES

Perhaps the most striking example of the manner in which modern firm-building in Tabanan reflects and depends upon traditional patterns of organization and loyalty is the development of what is today easily the town's largest and most important business concern, Gadarata (Gabungan Dagang Rakjat Tabanan — "The People's Trade Association of Tabanan"). Founded in 1945 by four local noblemen plus a long-resident Javanese market-trader, evidently as a technical advisor, the association amassed its Rp. 100,000 capital by levying a "contribution" of five rupiah on every household head in the area, each contributor being awarded a voting share in the projected enterprise.[19] Approximately 10,000 villagers bought a share, and the remaining Rp. 50,000 was raised by selling multiple shares to richer individuals, most, but not all of them, town aristocrats. (The number of shares

[19] The boundaries of the population appealed to are unclear, but neither the Swapradja, which was too large, nor the district, which was too small, as such, seem to have been the units. Rather, the riceland villages around Tabanan, where ties to the court have always been stronger, seem to have been mainly involved. As no legal enforcement, only traditional moral suasion, mixed with a certain amount of nationalist appeal, was employed, probably not all individuals complied. But the overwhelming majority seem to have done so.

one holder could own was unlimited, but no one person was allowed to cast more than six votes.) The plan was to funnel all export trade for the region through this one well-organized, incorporated, upper-caste-managed concern as agent, as well as to launch certain other associated business enterprises, and a large, two-story warehouse, store, and office building, the town's most imposing edifice, was erected at the main crossroads near the market.

Dutch occupation of the whole area during the Revolution limited Gadarata's activities fairly sharply, however, and it was only after the transfer of sovereignty in 1950 that the enterprise really got under way. The governing board, which by now had had two more strategic members of the ruling family added to it (the Javanese trader had withdrawn), reorganized the firm by changing the size of the shares from five to one hundred rupiah each, thereby reducing the total number of shares from around 20,000 to about 1,000 at a single blow. The individual household head shareholders in the village were thus forced into either selling out their interests to larger holders or banding together into "Gadarata *seka*" of twenty people each and selecting a representative to attend annual stockholder meetings and cast their vote. Altogether, about 350 such *seka* were formed — covering about 7,000 of the original 10,000 villagers — while the rest of the small owners sold out to the leadership group, which thus consolidated its hold on the firm through this whole process. In any case, from a capital of about Rp. 100,000 the enterprise had, by the end of 1957, become worth something over half a million and dominated much of the export trade of the area, a trade which had, in prewar times, been wholly in Chinese hands. By almost any standard, Gadarata has been a most successful undertaking.

By 1957 one of the mainstays of Gadarata was the "export" (i.e., any shipment outside the island) of coffee, for which it had been awarded an official local monopoly by the military government. (All of Indonesia was under martial law at this time.) Though smaller local businessmen are free to buy up coffee from the growers — who are mostly found in the mountain areas of northwestern Tabanan — they are obliged to sell it for export to

Gadarata at a legally fixed price. The firm also traded in pigs
and cattle, two of Bali's most promising and most profitable exports, as well as the less important cash crop products — soya bean,
copra, coconut oil — and it had concluded a contract with the
government to provide rice for all the jails in Bali.[20]

Aside from its export activities, Gadarata is active also as an
importer. It runs its own retail "general" store on the first floor
of its building, and also wholesales import goods to a number of
smaller, local, Balinese-owned stores. Aside from selling the usual
consumption goods — flashlights, stationery, textiles — the firm is
also agent for Dunlop tires (as there are no railways in Bali, all
important interlocal transport is by truck or bus), Royal Dutch
Shell kerosene, and West German cement, and is the only official
local distributor of East-Java-produced sugar. At one point, the
concern even invaded the industrial field, opening a semimecha-
nized soft-drink bottling factory and a soap factory; but there the
skills of its directors were evidently not suffiicient to prevail
against the already entrenched local Chinese, and the businesses
failed.

The firm now employs six clerks, four truck drivers, four permanent laborers, and usually has twenty to thirty occasional
laborers working for it at any one time. Over-all management
and policy-making is completely in the hands of seven salaried
directors, five of whom, including the chairman and vice-chairman, are members of the ruling family. The tendency for the firm
to come progressively under the control of the "palace" group,
so as to be more or less their private concern, has by now become
almost complete, and this fact is recognized, and for the most
part accepted, by aristocrats and villagers alike. The former com-
plain that diffused control makes for inefficiency and confusion,

[20] With the sudden rise in rice prices during the 1957–58 political crisis,
the concern actually lost money on this particular deal. In addition, the
extreme disruption of interisland shipping resulting from the precipitate na-
tionalization of the Royal Dutch Packet Company (KPM) in late 1957 threatened the firm and the whole Balinese economy; by the end of the research
period in mid-1958, the immediate future of Gadarata, as indeed of all Indonesia, was highly uncertain.

and small holders always want profits to be declared as dividends rather than reinvested in expansion (to date no dividends have ever been declared). The latter say that the directors pay no attention at all to the small shareholders, and whenever anyone is bold enough to inquire what has become of his investment he is shown paper profits. Despite a few more vocal, politicized urban critics, who voice their suspicions and complaints at the annual stockholders' meetings but do little else about them, the majority of the stockholders seem to accept this situation of upper-caste dominance as a more or less natural state of affairs. They do not expect to have any particular say in institutions focused around the nobility simply because they have provided capital, any more than they expected to influence state policy simply because they contributed work and material to the lord's ceremonies in the old days. The managerial revolution has come quickly to Tabanan — mainly because it involves no revolution.

In addition to Gadarata there is a similar, somewhat smaller, yet still substantial firm of this general sort in Tabanan — its offices and warehouse lying directly north of Gadarata's — called Ksatria. Organized in 1950, five years after the founding of Gadarata, it raised its starting capital by selling shares not to individuals but to hamlets as undivided units. Each such share sold for five hundred rupiah, which the hamlet had to raise as a group. The total capital thus accumulated came to Rp. 265,000, which, as again some of the shares were bought in lots by richer urbanites, means that about 350 hamlets participated. Lacking Gadarata's coffee monopoly, the export of copra and livestock has been the mainstay of this concern, along with the operation of the local gasoline station, a very profitable agency (Ksatria also tried a bottling works and also failed). In addition to its town warehouse, the concern has four branch warehouses in various outlying villages where most of the crop and livestock buying is done, owns three trucks, and employs about twenty-five clerks and laborers. Again, the ruling family dominates the board of directors, which operates more or less independently of the stockholders, with the present head coming from the same noble house as the present head of Gadarata, who is his full patri-cousin, while the vice-chairman is a member of a large commoner house which historically acted as a major arm of royal power.[21]

Both Gadarata and Ksatria, then, show fairly clearly the manipulation both of traditional *seka*-type horizontal ties and of vertical politico-religious loyalties in the interest of modern economic ends. In these two firms at least (a third such firm, organized in a similar manner, failed after a few years of operation), the pattern of mass support of large-scale, noble-centered undertakings persists, only now these undertakings are concerned with extra-local trade rather than war or ceremony. A slightly different, yet generally similar, example of upper-caste leadership in modern economic matters is given by the rather more individualistic activities of the present Lord of Krambitan, a traditional ruler turned entrepeneur, par excellence.

Krambitan lies some fifteen kilometers southwest of Tabanan, and though its ruling family is a branch of the Tabanan royal line and its lord has always owed direct allegiance to the Lord of Tabanan, the area formed, in precolonial times, a fairly independent and at least partially autonomous political unit. Landholdings, military allegiances, economic and ceremonial ties all tended, rather atypically, to coalesce within the immediate region in such a way as to make a Krambitan a kind of subkingdom within Tabanan as a whole. Until 1955 the present lord, who is only thirty-two, was, as became customary under the Dutch, district officer for Krambitan. But when the Lord of Tabanan abdicated, this man, an individual of prodigious energies and large ideas, abdicated with him, and, in disgust, turned his interest away from political life to launch a whole series of highly successful business enterprises ranging from a hotel to a tire-recapping factory.[22]

---

[21] Thiis commoner house, despite its lack of actual genealogical connection, is a part of the royal complex in both its own eyes and those of the population generally. Such houses, often particularly favored by the king as a counterweight to the various branches of his own family, are found in almost all Balinese kingdoms, and they often achieve a great deal of independent political power.

[22] The Lord of Tabanan, still the area's "king" in the eyes of most Tabananers, has himself become a hotelkeeper since his retirement from political life, as well as engaging in various trading activities.

The tire-recapping factory, located at the eastern edge of Tabanan town, is perhaps the best example of this man's boldness, ingenuity, and ability to fuse traditional political and modern economic patterns into a single whole. As already mentioned, almost all important commercial transport in Bali takes place by truck or bus. The Lord of Krambitan noting that, despite this reliance on motor transport, all tire casings had to be sent by ship to Java for recapping, an expensive and time consuming process, decided that here was an opportunity just waiting to be grasped. He traveled to the large Javanese cities of Surabaja and Djakarta to observe recapping plants there and judge the possibility of founding such a plant in Bali. In Djakarta he came into contact with a Chinese concern which owned seven such plants. Assuring himself, for legal as well as patriotic reasons, that the Chinese involved were Indonesian and not Chinese citizens, he proposed a deal to them. They would provide 20 per cent of the Rp. 250,000 capital needed, obtain the machines, insure a steady supply of rubber, and instruct a group of his Krambitan dependents how to operate a recap factory: he and his brother-in-law (who, as the Balinese upper castes are highly endogamous, is also his cousin) would provide 30 per cent of the capital each, insure a disciplined and responsible labor force, and, through the lord's political contacts on Bali, secure a government-protected, island-wide monopoly for the industry. At length, the Chinese agreed: a partnership was formed, the plant set up. By mid-1958 the industry had been running with apparent smoothness for over a year, and the two Chinese who had directed operations in the initial phases had long since returned to Djakarta leaving things entirely in Balinese hands.

The productive process itself is not too demanding technically, despite the various sorts of machinery involved, the main requirement being care that impurities do not get into the rubber. At present, fourteen men, all traditional commoner dependents of the lord, work in the factory, each being assigned to a particular phase of the process — scraping old casings, applying the new rubber, pressing the cap in the machine — and the brother-in-law acts as day-to-day manager and work foreman. Rubber is shipped regularly from Djakarta (or was until the disruption of inter-island shipping during the civil war), the site is owned by the lord and rented from him by the company, and a Chinese-owned auto-parts store in Den Pasar acts as the concern's sole retail agent. Working on a regularized, assembly-line type of schedule, the workers, who a year ago were landless share-tenants, can recap from seven to ten tires a day. But both the lord and his Chinese partners are planning to expand production considerably as time passes, for the local market is nowhere near being adequately served by the present output.

As noted, this man has not confined his entrepreneurial activities to one enterprise. He buys and sells automobiles, which have what can only be called a peculiar, almost obsessive fascination for him, at a tremendous rate. He has restored some of the more traditional parts of his palace and polished up some of his heirlooms in the hope, so far unfulfilled, of attracting to Krambitan some of the tourist traffic which now goes mainly eastward from Den Pasar, and has even attempted to talk a national film company into making a film there in order to publicize Krambitan's attractions. In partnership with his paternal uncle he owns a four-bus bus line, running from Krambitan to Tabanan. He owns a five-thousand-rupiah share — as does another member of his immediate family — in a large Den Pasar trading concern with a branch in Surabaja. And he has built a new hotel in Tabanan, which is managed by one of his three wives (a second minds the palace and the third teaches school) and, like the bus line, staffed with commoner Krambitan dependents. All together, the lord's enterprises give work to more than fifty men, and, in fact, although he is not so hypocritical as to deny that he is vitally interested in making money, he gives as one of his major motivations in trying to launch new businesses the desire to meet his traditional obligation to provide support for his needy subjects and so maintain his customary status in their eyes. It is the central government's failure to comprehend what he regards as the special characteristics of his position that most inflames him about "modern politics" (and politicians) and which has forced him to think of new ways to legitimize an old role:

He complained about all the taxes he has to pay [on his land] now. He has lots of traditional dependents to support, servants to maintain, and so on. And he has to give many large ceremonies. Aristocrats have to have large ceremonies, other people skimp, but they cannot, they have to have elaborate ones because the people expect it of individuals in their position. But the tax office doesn't understand this sort of thing. It just says that the aristocrats are leading the good life and taxes their income as such, failing to realize that they have fixed obligations, descending for generations, to all kinds of dependents and that this takes a lot of their money. If a man comes to the palace and needs work, he must give him some, and the local peasantry has always counted on the palace to tide them over in bad times. This is why he has gone into trade. So far he is the only one in his family who has done a great deal along these lines, but his young nephew has just graduated from business high school in Java and should soon begin to achieve something in trade.

Except for a Rp. 50,000 loan from a government bank to pay for part of his Rp. 300,000 hotel, the Lord of Krambitan has raised all his capital by selling riceland, of which he (or his family) was, until he began his shift from landlord to big businessman, one of the region's most substantial holders. At first his family strongly resisted selling riceland, and he actually sold off a good deal of it surreptitiously to begin with, without informing his mother. When she discovered what he had been doing she was, he says, appalled and said he was dissipating the family fortune, trading in sacred heirlooms, and would bring ruin on them all. But by then the hotel was built, and he took her to Tabanan and had her live there and watch the money come in for a while. She was ultimately converted to his point of view, eagerly supporting his later effort in the tire factory.

Another example of largely individual aristocratic entrepreneurship — though of a more circumscribed and rather special sort — is the founding by a Tabanan noble of a weaving factory in which all the twenty-five weavers were women of the ruling family itself — i.e., wives, sisters, and daughters of the various lords and lordlings. Weaving, particularly of the finer, luxury textiles

has long been a specialty, in precolonial times virtually a monopoly, of the royal and priestly (i.e., Brahmana) families. The large
houses with their surpluses of idle women (the surplus was a result of large-scale polygamy; the idleness, of large staffs of servants
combined with a belief that noble women ought not to appear
in public except in emergencies) made of the weaving of cloth
a specialized craft which it was both proper and admirable, even
requisite, for an upper-caste woman to pursue. And this pattern
continues, in diminished form, today; in many noble and priestly
houses the women still pass the hours weaving the finely textured,
gold-and-silver-threaded shawls and sarongs of traditional Bali.
It was on this tradition that the entrepreneur — who had necessarily to be a noble himself — drew. But he drew on it in a novel
form, introducing crucial innovations into the whole process. He
brought the women out of their harems into a factory, provided
them with improved looms imported from Java, set them on a
regular schedule, paid them on a piecework basis, and converted
them from weaving fine and expensive textiles for the elite to
producing cheap sarongs for the masses.

The factory ran for three years, the entrepreneur handling the
business end of things, his wife acting as work supervisor over the
weavers. Fifteen to twenty sarongs were produced daily and were
sold either to local stores or market-traders on a commission basis.
For the first three years the industry ran smoothly and profits
steadily grew, but deteriorating business conditions forced the
entrepreneur to close the shop down — temporarily, he claims —
at the end of the fourth year. The entrepreneur gives two main
reasons for his inability to keep the industry going. The first is
that all the thread, which comes from Japan, is imported in Java
by Chinese and Arabs who also own weaving factories of their
own. He claims that these people, to discourage competition, deliberately keep the price of thread as high as possible to independent weavers, particularly in an area such as Bali which is a prime
market for the textile manufacturers of eastern Java. During the
Ali Sastroamidjojo cabinets, which were committed to "Indo-
nesianizing" the domestic economy, the industry bureau of the
Finance Ministry distributed thread on a quota basis at fixed

prices, but when these cabinets fell, importing was set free again and the resultant squeeze put him out of business. He and a few other Balinese would-be textile-entrepreneurs are trying to get the government to appoint an official thread importer in Bali, say Gadarata for Tabanan; or at least to forbid concerns which own looms to import thread too. If this is done, the entrepreneur is convinced that he can once again make a go of his industry, which he says has not failed but is only "resting," and he is very eager to do so. (The factory is intact and production could be resumed within a week.)

The second reason he gives for his difficulties is that with the increasing population in the villages and the general deterioration of economic conditions in Indonesia as a whole in the last five years, fewer and fewer peasants are planting dry season cash crops, but instead are double-cropping rice which is mainly self-consumed, so that there is less cash in the villages now than there was before 1954. Whether these reasons for the closing, permanent or temporary, of his firm are valid or not — and the comments about Chinese business practices are probably not entirely a matter of prejudice — his enterprise shows quite clearly the integration of traditional and modern elements (though in this case wholly intramural to the ruling family) within one economic institution which is the essence of economic innovation and development in contemporary Tabanan.

Yet another, more broadly based, sort of half-traditional, half-modern business concern is the Den Pasar-Tabanan-Gilimanuk bus line centered in Tabanan. Headed and organized by the town's main automobile garage owner and mechanic, who is again an aristocrat (of the same house, actually, as the weaving-factory owner), this concern, which is unincorporated, is more of a voluntary *seka* than it is a true firm. It was formed in 1952 by fourteen occasional bus-drivers and mechanics (eleven of them commoners) in order to secure the concession from the government of the profitable route from the island capital to the terminal of the ferry which plies the two-mile strait between Gilimanuk and the Javanese town of Banjuwangi. Eleven of the drivers put up Rp. 5,000 each, the entrepreneur and two others put up Rp. 10,000, for a total capital of Rp. 85,000.[23] Most of these drivers raised their own contributions by selling or pawning riceland. They had been part-time replacement drivers for other owners, and part-time farmers and wished to become fully professional drivers with their own buses, and so abandoned their interests in landholding and the peasant economy to achieve this aim.

The *seka* began by purchasing three buses on the instalment plan from a local Chinese, costing in total about Rp. 100,000, and has prospered; today, it owns nine. The entrepreneur provides his equipment and garage for minor repairs of the buses — which are necessary very frequently because of the state of Balinese roads — to the *seka* without cost, charging only for major repair work. The administrative duties involved are also performed without pay — the entrepreneur handles the technical end, one of the members takes care of the accounting, and another does the scheduling. The drivers and the conductors (the latter not being members of the *seka*) are paid a monthly salary, and so far all profits have been used to buy more buses. Again, the upper-caste keystone of this whole enterprise sees his function, quite honestly, almost as much in terms of creating jobs as of earning profits, his main personal income coming from his thriving garage business (which in itself employs eight people). Every bus, he says, means three times that many jobs for people — two conductors and a driver. Also the school children wash the buses and various other people make part of a living from them in one way or another. All in all, this enterprise obviously rests on concepts of group loyalty and traditional leadership which grow directly out of rural social organization and which are wholly lacking in the bazaar economy.

Finally, by far the most impressive and most fully developed business firm in Tabanan is the Airlangga Ice Factory, in which the pattern of noble entrepreneurship reaches a climax for this region. The factory — a large white building near the eastern end of the town — was organized in 1952 by four nobles and the Java-

---

[23] One member later quit, and a second was ejected for corruption. Both of these men were given back their capital, so there are now only twelve members and Rp. 75,000 basic capital.

nese owner of a local motion picture theater. The group is headed by one of the nobles, the son of the chief of irrigation for all Tabanan — about the last of the high traditional officials still in office in the Swapradja [24] — who saw in the fact that all the ice consumed locally had to be brought in from Den Pasar twenty miles away an opportunity for a profitable local enterprise. The group also includes the present head of Gadarata and the weaving-factory entrepreneur. Capital was raised through the sale of thirty Rp. 10,000 shares, plus about Rp. 200,000 in loans from peasants, small urban businessmen, and local civil servants.[25] Of the thirty stockholders, sixteen, including the above-mentioned founders, as well as the Lord of Krambitan and the head of Ksatria, were members of the ruling family, four were lesser, unrelated, upper-caste people, two were Javanese bazaar-traders, five were commoner *seka* (one of which includes over a hundred members), two were business firms (Gadarata and a Den Pasar trading concern of a similar type in which the ice factory founder also has an interest), and one was an individual commoner.[26] The head of the founding group

[24] This office, that of *Sedahan Agung,* had in the prewar period a political importance rivaled only by that of king itself. Himself a major lord, the *Sedahan Agung* was responsible for all matters having to do with irrigation not capable of being handled at the level of the individual irrigation society, as well as administering the land tax. This particular man retired in 1957 and was replaced by a non-noble professional civil servant, the first time the office has been held by an individual not of the royal family. In most parts of Bali, however, particularly in the more traditional eastern areas, the nobility still monopolizes the local administrative apparatus. In these areas, too, the entrepreneurial dynamic of the more displaced Tabanan aristocrats is also generally lacking.

[25] The willingness of at least some peasants to lend money to urban businesses offers a sharp contrast to the situation in Modjokuto, where this is quite rare. Not only the ice factory, but both Gadarata and Ksatria, as well as some smaller enterprises, have borrowed money on the "open market" in Tabanan. Some peasants even go so far as to pawn some of their land, invest the money in an urban business, and use the resultant interest payments to maintain their children in a town secondary school. One of the main reasons the aristocrats give for the preponderance of their kind on the governing boards of urban enterprises is that it is only when the peasant sees such traditional figures heading a concern that he will be willing to lend money to it.

[26] There are, at least on the surface, no multiple holdings. The company itself has since bought up the share of the Javanese theater owner, who has died.

became director of the firm, the weaving entrepreneur vice-director (the only two salaried managers), and a government monopoly for Tabanan and the neighboring Swapradja to the west, Djembrana, was secured. In the first two years of operation the industry lost Rp. 3,000 and Rp. 15,000; but in its third, fourth, and fifth years it showed profits of Rp. 16,000, Rp. 20,000, and (estimated) Rp. 80,000, so that, after a slow start, it has become a going concern.

The factory itself is capital intensive for Indonesia, employing only about ten laborers altogether. The machinery, which includes large water tanks, a complicated piping system, ammonia pumps, a diesel-driven compressor, and so on, cost nearly Rp. 400,000 (land and housing for the factory accounting for most of the rest of the original capital) and was imported via a Dutch concern in Surabaja from England and Holland. Output averages about two metric tons of block ice a day, and sales are made early each morning to hundreds of itinerant bazaar peddlers who take only a few rupiahs' worth of crushed ice and sell it, in ten or twenty-five-cents glassfuls (usually with some syrup poured on it for flavor) in the villages or the streets of the town. The cry of the ice peddler is one of the commonest and most welcome sounds of present day Bali, and as in the case of Modjokuto's more modern enterprises it is a crucial and widespread shift in tastes which has made this novel sort of economic activity profitable at all:

He [the vice-director] said ice selling has been much less affected by the money shortage in the villages than has textile selling. He said this was a result of "progress." Before the war there was only one, Chinese-owned, ice factory for all Bali in Den Pasar, and it was not very big. Only aristocrats and Dutchmen drank ice; not the peasant. The peasant never drank ice or soda pop. Now we have progress and everybody drinks it. Before, if people went down to the ocean, for example, for an outing, they brought several young coconuts and drank the juice of them. Now, with more schooling, outside influence and so on, probably 90 per cent will drink soda pop or ice. Lots of ice is sold in the villages now and people will buy ice before they buy clothes. Ice is like cigarettes now, he said: you have to buy it, it is a necessity not a luxury.

People, for example, ask if there is ice before they go into a coffee shop nowadays, and if there is no ice they won't go there to eat their rice. Also, ice is very cheap, only a few cents a drink, and every day people drink a little of it so that it has become part of their everyday life; people drink more regularly than they eat now. When the bus drivers go off on their long hot trips, they all drink ice; if they didn't they wouldn't be able to stand the strain. . . .

The moving spirit of this enterprise — the son of the irrigation chief — is like the Lord of Krambitan, a man of many interests, extraordinary energy, and highly developed ambitions. (Like him, also, he is an only child; something of a rarity in Bali.) Not only was he one of the founders of Gadarata, but he has opened a retail store selling imported goods and foodstuffs in front of the house to which he belongs, and has begun to engage in independent crop and livestock buying for export on his own. And, like the Lord of Krambitan, he quite consciously sees himself as shifting the material basis of his family's eminence from land ownership and political power to commerce and industry, as maintaining an old ascendancy in a new society:

He began talking, without any prompting from me, about the noble houses and business. He said that aristocrats, such as himself, were changing the foundations of their economy. Before the war their wealth rested on political power and rice-field ownership. But now the politicians are pushing the aristocrats out of political power and confiscatory taxes are ruining larger landholders. Now we get taxed two or three times a year. Before the war the taxes were all in our favor; that's how we got rich — I admit it — because we had the government. No we don't have it any more and the taxes are against us, which is I suppose fair enough. The result is that people like me are saying: "They've taken the government away from us; all right, we'll capture the economy." . . . If your wealth is in riceland, you only get half the crop anyway, the other half goes to the tenant; and tomorrow, the way things are going, it may be two-thirds. The government is always thinking up new regulations to protect the tenant, but never the landlord. Also your wealth is more obvious in landholding than in commerce. Further, the noble families are growing in size and they can't live off riceland alone any more. While at the same time more and more aristocrats are giving up wanting to be civil servants any more, in disgust with the political situation; almost nobody in the government offices any more has any experience. Thus, everyone is going into business. I asked whether the aristocrats didn't look upon trade as demeaning and he said no, there was no feeling of that sort. Before the war no aristocrats were in trade at all, but now there is not only no prejudice against it but, indeed, people are more enthusiastic about it than the civil service. He himself started out in agricultural school with the idea of succeeding his father as irrigation chief, but quit finally to go into business where he felt there was more of a future.

Clearly, then, the heart of Tabanan's post-Revolutionary economic expansion has been a relatively small group of displaced and threatened traditional rulers. In addition to the firms mentioned above, there are two general stores, a tailor shop and "school," a bookstore, and a smaller export concern, run by aristocrats. Also, most of this upper-caste, entrepreneurial group has formed a co-operative bank — headed by the ice-factory founder, the weaving entrepreneur, the head of Gadarata, and the government official in charge of the market (also a member of the ruling family, cousin to the weaving entrepreneur)— which makes short-term (three to six months) loans up to Rp. 2,000 for trading purposes at an interest rate of 2 per cent for the term, a very low rate for Indonesia, and which clearly further strengthens the interlocking directorate quality of this whole development. Of course, as there are some non-trader *prijaji* entrepreneurs in Modjokuto so there are in Tabanan several smaller commoner-owned stores, one fairly substantial commoner-run shoe shop, and more Balinese, all of them commoners, sell in the market than ever before. In general, though, the above selection of enterprises has not been purposely biased, but covers all the main Balinese-owned firms which exist: Tabanan's traditional ruling family — about 6 per cent of its population — overwhelmingly dominates the nascent modern economy of the town.[27]

[27] This is not to say that they are all as one. There are, within this group, a great many internal conflicts, rivalries, and the like, some of them tracing

Upper-Caste Revolution and the Limits of Tradition

If, for a moment, we look at Tabanan's developmental pattern against the background of Modjokuto's, certain of its distinctive characteristics emerge in bolder relief. Such a comparison can be conducted in terms of four interrelated theoretical concerns: (1) an evaluation of modern economic activities in the two towns in terms of types and effectiveness of the organizational forms through which they are expressed, (2) a delineation of the contrasting religious and ideological dynamics of development in both places, (3) an investigation of the implications of an essentially politically based and oriented developmental process as against an essentially trade-based and oriented one, and (4) a discussion of differential degrees of urbanization with respect to economic growth. This fourfold analysis of similarities and differences can serve to summarize the essential nature of Tabanan's "upper-caste revolution," as well as lead to a preliminary assessment of its longer run prospects.

In organizational terms there is little doubt that the firms of Tabanan are much more impressive than those of Modjokuto. The bringing together of hundreds of villages in a common effort of the Gadarata or Ksatria sort does not even seem to be a realistic alternative to a Modjokuto entrepreneur. Not only does he entirely lack the traditional prestige to mobilize people on such a scale, but nearly three hundred years of intensive, Western-stimulated social change in Java have eroded the foundations for large-scale collective effort in the villages, particularly in so highly monetized a former plantation area as Modjokuto where the overwhelming majority of peasants — if they can be called peasants at all — are really independent, cash-crop farmers, tenants, or agricultural laborers, dealing almost completely in terms of

far back in history, which should be investigated in detail. Some noble houses, and some branches within such houses, are very active, others not at all. All these people are in a broad sense related to one another, but the economic unit is the elementary or slightly extended patrilineal family, not the whole noble house, much less the whole ruling "lineage." Though, like Modjokuto's pious Reform Moslem traders, Tabanan's entrepreneurial aristocrats form a definite and well-demarcated group, the internal integration of that group ought not to be overemphasized.

the market. A goodly amount of mutual aid does occur, of course, in the Modjokuto countryside, but there is nothing even remotely resembling the *seka* pattern of pluralistic collectivism; most co-operation is between two or three neighbors, friends, or kin, and tends to be sporadic and situational rather than persistent and institutionalized. And, too, Modjokuto's entrepreneurs emerge directly from a bazaar economy in which individualistic, every-man-for-himself activity is carried almost to an extreme in con-trast to the lineage-like organization of the relatively solidary and corporate ruling family from which Tabanan's new men come.

As a result, almost all Modjokuto's modern enterprises are indi-vidual or immediate family concerns, and capital must be raised either through personal savings or (increasingly) through govern-ment loans; selling shares to villagers or large-scale borrowing on the open market is virtually absent, for the peasant's deep-grained suspicion of traders effectively prohibits any relation between the two save that of the customary semihostile commerce. In Mod-jokuto even partnerships, so easily formed in Tabanan, where strong non-economic ties of kinship, coresidence, or status defer-ence usually insure their persistence, are almost non-existent, though there are a few — for example, the hat factory. When it comes to the organizational problem, then Tabananers have a clear advantage, for the cultural tradition upon which they draw provides ready-made forms for collective activity of a specialized sort, whereas that upon which the Modjokutans draw does not.

Yet there is another side to the coin, reflected in the constant complaint of their directors that the popularly based large firms are unwieldy and inefficient, as well as in the constant effort of these directors to concentrate control in fewer and fewer hands. In part, this is simply economic man talking, because the hands they speak of are of course their own; but in part it is a realistic assessment. Especially as national-political concerns come to have more importance, there is a tendency for them to penetrate these supposedly specifically economic institutions and cause consider-able internal disruption, something the individualistic Modjo-kuto entrepreneur completely avoids. Cast in quasi-political terms to begin with, Tabanan's firms can become easily politicized in modern terms and this is — at least in a democratic state — extremely·disfunctional to further growth or even to continued solvency. Second, and perhaps even more important, the popularly based concern has a tendency to behave uneconomically because of the "social welfare" pressures of its members who, for the most part, are not basically growth-minded. Not only is there great pressure to divide profits rather than reinvest them, but there is also a tendency to employ overly large staffs in an attempt by the directorate to appease the rank and file. It was this too-many-cooks sort of pressure which may have caused the failure of one large trading concern and which did affect Gadarata, and particularly Ksatria, adversely. The trouble with Balinese-owned concerns, the abdicated king of Tabanan, who runs his hotel by himself, said to me with some shrewdness, is that they turn into relief organizations rather than businesses. "If you go into one of them," he said, "there are a half-dozen directors, a bookkeeper or two, several clerks, some truckdrivers and a hoard of semi-idle workers; if you go into a Chinese concern of the same size there is just the proprietor, his wife, and his ten-year-old boy, but they are getting even more work done." And the founder of the ice company (who thinks that even its thirty members are too many for effective functioning), responded to a question about co-operatives with genuine horror:

> It is much better in a business to have one or two men running things than having everybody participating and putting in his views. The government is always urging co-ops on them, but he thought they just led to those who knew something about trade being dominated by a great number of people who were poor in knowledge but rich in opinions. He said this was true of "collective" business generally, such as Gadarata; the people who really know what they are doing are smothered by the inexperienced, who are more interested in getting an immediate and certain gain than taking risks and seeing the business succeed.

In miniature, the contrast here is one between what A. O. Hirschman, speaking of developmental ideologies in underdeveloped countries in general has called a "group focused image of change" *vs.* an "ego focused image of change." [28] In the first sort of conception "Individuals will think of economic change as something that must affect equally all members of the group with which they identify themselves. The idea of change then transforms the 'image' of a stationary society where everybody plays his [traditionally] assigned role into one of a progressive or dynamic society with the individuals remaining at their previous places in relation to the group." [29] This is the Tabanan noble-plus-*seka* approach: economic change does not alter the organizational forms of pluralistic collectivism in any fundamental way, it merely applies them to new ends; the form of society is constant, only its content changes.

In the second sort of image of change, that which has dominated the literature on development since Schumpeter and the (American) popular mind since Henry Ford, ". . . economic progress . . . may be conceived as possible [and beckoning] for the individual while it is not visualized at all for the group. The individual . . . who is brought face to face with the evidence of [the possibility for] economic progress will reinterpret it to mean that he can improve his own lot [but] will dismiss such possibility for society as a whole simply because not identifying himself with society he will relate new experiences to himself alone." [30] This is, more or less, the Modjokuto pattern: each entrepreneur is out for his own interests and expects others, as far as they are enlightened, to be out for theirs. He is pioneering and, as a pioneer, he expects to be on his own; under the intense stimulation of nationalistic ideologies about building a non-colonial economy, insofar as he does become concerned to conceptualize the problem of development in the economy generally, he sees it vaguely and indifferently in terms of the steady growth of independent businesses like his own, and of the steady, spontaneous multiplication of self-propelled merchants and manufacturers like himself.

As Hirschman also points out, both of these approaches to

[28] A. O. Hirschman, *The Strategy of Economic Development* (New Haven, Conn.: Yale University Press, 1958), pp. 11 ff.

[29] *Ibid.*, p. 12.

[30] *Ibid.*, p. 14.

change have their defects and their virtues. The group-focused approach, speaking now of Tabanan in particular, smooths the way to the formation of large-scale concerns while, at the same time, traditional values supporting collective benefits as against individual enrichment induce a strong resistance to the rationalization of these concerns once they are formed. This is not a matter of simple egalitarianism — for, as we have noted, both the commoner and the noble accept the latter's right both to make his own policy decisions without consultation with his followers and also to take the lion's share of the returns as a traditional prerogative; but what *both* commoner and noble expect and demand, both of each other and themselves, is that these decisions will lead to a higher level of welfare for the organic community as a whole and not just to an enrichment of a self-interested, emergent managerial class. Relative inequality may and should persist — Bali is hardly an egalitarian society — but should not be transformed into new and different kind of inequality. We have seen this outlook in almost everyone of our entrepreneurs: modern economic activity is in great part an attempt to maintain old, agrarian-based patterns of paternalistic support on the one hand and deferential dependence on the other. And among the peasants, the same image holds: the large collective firms should be noble-run enterprises dedicated to the welfare of all, each according to his status, much as were the wars and ceremonies of old. Although in many ways admirable from a short-run ethical standpoint, and offering many immediate first-stage organizational advantages, this essentially conservative kind of approach to change can be very inhibiting to long-run development when perfect "parity" is impossible to maintain.

The ego-focused approach of Modjokuto avoids most of these particular problems. The emergence of new relationships between classes and groups is accepted, as are the prospects of other fundamental changes in society; personal enrichment is considered a reasonable goal for an individual to pursue; [31] and Modjokuto

[31] These and the following remarks pertain mainly to the truly urbanized elements in Modjokuto and in particular to the pious Moslem trading group. Among the peasantry and the traditional elements in the civil service there is still a strong group-focused approach to change which has similar effects

entrepreneurs are able to sweat labor far beyond anything a Balinese can yet achieve. No one expects a Modjokuto storekeeper or manufacturer to make decisions in other than economic terms. He has in abundance the classic free-enterprise virtue of the rational pursuit of self-interest, and he is the type of "look out for number one" sort of man whom an American small businessman of the first half of the twentieth century could completely understand, his egoism tempered by an Islamic charity ethic as the American's was by a Protestant one.

Despite the advantages of such bold and rugged, not to say ruthless, individualism in stimulating creativity and destroying customary constraints on enterprise in a traditional society, it seems that, ethical considerations apart, it also involves very important limitations on the capacity to grow, by limiting the effective range of collective organization. Modjokuto enterprises seem to grow so large and then no larger, because the next step means widening the social base of the enterprise beyond the immediate family connections to which, given that lack of trust which is the inverse of individualism, they are limited. Where Tabanan's group-focused approach tends to expand firms beyond their most efficient organizational base, Modjokuto's ego-centered one tends to confine them to too narrow a one, and this, too, is likely to form an increasingly serious barrier to growth as time passes.[32]

It is, of course, just the sort of weak and evasive conclusion all-too-typical of social scientists to say that effective growth demands just so much group-focus and just so much ego-focus, but not too

on the few enterprises launched by these less dynamic groups as it has in Tabanan. See my comments on "shared poverty," in "Religious Belief and Economic Behavior in a Central Javanese Town," *Economic Development and Cultural Change*, IV, No. 2 (1956). The promulgation of an intense nationalistic rhetoric of the group-focused type also complicates the problem, for even the most self-oriented Modjokuto businessman is obliged to utter clichés about his social motivations and values, and this ethic tends to lead to an even greater general devaluation of the businessman than that already induced by his generally "interstitial" position.

[32] For an extreme case of ego-focus which effectively inhibits any significant economic growth at all see Edward C. Banfield, *The Moral Basis of a Backward Society* (Glencoe, Ill.: Free Press, 1958).

much or too little of either; but in the case of the Tabanan-
Modjokuto contrast, nothing more circumstantial can be said.
Tabanan's group approach, its pluralistic collectivism, gives it
advantages in mobilizing capital, disadvantages in improving
efficiciency and rationality; Modjokuto's ego approach, its bazaar-
economy individualism, gives it advantages in efficiency, disadvantages in capitalization. In a sense, both towns are dealing with
the same organizational problem — how to construct fully modern
economic firms which can strike the most productive balance between the free operation of individual initiative and a broad base
of group support — but they are coming at it from diametrically
opposed positions. In Tabanan, group support is not problematical, the free operation of individual initiative is; in Modjokuto the
reverse is true. Where development in the Balinese town is threatened by an overdevelopment of collective organization, in the
Javanese it is threatened by an underdevelopment of it.

Our second contrast, the religious and ideological one, is more
straightforward. In Modjokuto, the entrepreneur mainly follows
a discordant, rationalized, and self-consciously critical religious
creed — Islamic modernism — which sets him apart from his much
less devout and zealous fellows and which, in its very nature,
makes economic achievement ethically significant.[33] Although
there are important differences which a fuller study would need
to treat in detail, the Modjokuto shopkeeper's piety places him in
the same sort of moral tension with society around him in which
that of the English nonconformists placed them with theirs, and
offers him, through the ethical justification of secular economic
activity, the same type of resolution of that tension which evan-
gelical Protestantism provided them. The too often mooted question whether this sort of dynamic inner-worldly asceticism is a
cause or a consequence of the economic growth with which it has
been so often associated is beside the point (for, as social change
is systematic, it is actually both): what is crucial is that the counter-
traditional ideological orientation of Modjokuto's small business-

[33] For the "protestant ethic" element in modernist Islamic ideology in Indonesia see R. L. Archer, "Muhammedan Mysticism in Sumatra," *Journal of
the Royal Asiatic Society, Asian Branch*, CV, No. 2 (1937), pp. 1–126.

men puts them in the position of being not only economic but also religious and ethical innovators, and this is most definitely not true of the leaders of Tabanan's development. The religious beliefs and values of these latter, far from clashing with those of the general society, are rather the most elaborate, developed, and systematic expression of the culture's traditionally institutional ethos.

Thus, both marked deviation from the main stream of traditional religious thought and complete conformity to it seem able to provide an ideological context suitable for growth, because, so far as a stimulus to economic enterprise is concerned, what is important is not whether a creed is revisionist or restorationist but whether there is a significant degree of tension in the state of affairs the creed celebrates, the moral order it supports, and the perception of the actual situation the entrepreneurs have — their assessment of the way things really are. In Modjokuto, the pious shopkeepers see themselves as modern Moslems in a generally heterodox, old-fashioned religious community — the vanguard of a truly Islamic Indonesia. In Tabanan, the nobility sees itself as displaced from its true position as cultural cynosure, fighting to maintain the traditional patterns of deference, respect, and reverence upon which it feels the intrinsic value of Balinese culture rests. In both cases there is a gap between a vision of the way things ought to be and the way they seem to be, or to be fast becoming in a situation which rarely, if ever, occurs in stable traditional societies. What Modjokuto's aggressive petty bourgeois Moslem modernists and Tabanan's haughty Hinduized aristocrats share — and on an ideological level they share little else — is a troubled sense that the immediate social fate of the value system to which they are totally committed is very much in doubt. And it is out of this deep spiritual restlessness that much of their dynamism comes.

Third, where Modjokuto's developmental process is primarily economically oriented and based, that of Tabanan is fundamentally political; the Javanese entrepreneurs want mainly to become rich, the Balinese to become, or remain, powerful. The fact that economic development may, in many cases, be primarily politically rather than economically motivated has often been obscured by "liberal" interpretations of economic growth in western Europe, which have seen it as an outcome of the natural propensity of economic man to "truck, barter, and exchange" in unending search for personal profit, a propensity only hampered and interfered with by actions of positive government. But with analyses of later processes of industrialization, especially in Russia and Japan, the role of political goals and political values has come to be seen as more dynamic:

> Thus both the [Meiji] Restoration and the subsequent modernization of Japan must be seen first in political terms and only secondarily in economic terms. I am insistent on this point because the tendency to regard economic developments as "basic" and political developments as "superstrucrture" is by no means confined to Marxist circles but permeates most current thinking on such matters. Modernization, however, though it includes the notions of modernization of government, as well as education, medicine, etc., is so heavily dependent on economic factors that it is almost synonymous with industrialization. It is poor logic to draw from this the conclusion that the motivation for modernization must be primarily economic. Actually it seems clear that a great deal of motivation for modernization in Japan was political rather than economic, concerned with the increase of power, for which the increase of wealth was but a means.[34]

Tabanan's entrepreneurs, in contrast to Modjokuto's, have come from a class long used to wielding power, to feeling themselves the primary movers and shakers in their tight little cultural world. Born to the purple — though in Bali the color is yellow — they have not lost the confidence that comes with the effective exercise of political power on a large scale, the sense of personal potency which results when men jump to do one's bidding. The comparable class in Modjokuto — the civil servant *prijaji* — have for one hundred and fifty years been reduced to non-policymaking petty bureaucrats, white-collar errand boys of the Dutch crown, and have long since lost their original sense of playing a decisive role in their society. With the executive element in their elite

[34] R. Bellah, *Tokugawa Religion* (Glencoe, Ill.: Free Press, 1957), p. 185.

status, the substance of power, appropriated by the Dutch, they have developed talents of adjustment, accommodation, compromise, and refined acquiescence rather than of resolute and forceful leadership. This is one — among others — of the reasons they have not emerged in Modjokuto, or in most other parts of Java, as a strong entrepreneurial class.[35] The fact that Tabanan's ruling family maintained the realities of its sovereignty until 1906, and to a significant extent even after that year, is certainly one of the reasons for the vigor it shows in actively coping with the realities of the "new Indonesia," in contrast to the passive, disheartened, almost withdrawn reaction of their Modjokuto counterparts.[36]

Thus, in Tabanan the taste for economic innovation grows out of an aristocratic, even arrogant, sense of the individual entrepreneur's consciousness of being a man born to lead, while in Modjokuto it grows out of the individual entrepreneur's sense of his superior shrewdness, toughness, flexibility and ambition as contrasted to the passive, acceptant traditionalism of the ignorant or overcivilized clods around him. The bazaar economy breeds a man fast on his feet, one who values cleverness, resiliency, and the aggressive ability to go out and get what he wants in a social environment not at all inclined to yield it as a matter of course. From the plantation days until the present the successful business man in Modjokuto has been self-made; he has not been an established political figure exercising his unquestioned right to lead, but a semioutcast peddler making capital out of his quicker wit, directness, and relative lack of concern with customary amenities, obligations, and social surfaces, and his ingrained ability to keep his eye firmly fixed upon the business in hand. He is,

[35] The partial exception to this rule lies in the person of Sultan Hamenku Buwono IX of Jogjakarta, a central Javanese court town where the aristocracy has remained strong. The sultan, still the official head of administration in the Jogjakarta region, though now as chief of the local civil service bureaucracy, has taken the lead in stimulating a certain amount of locally basic economic growth. See Selosoemardjan, *Social Change in Jogjakarta* (Ithaca: Cornell University Press, 1962).

[36] Of course, properly speaking, Modjokuto has never had any ruling family at all. The Dutch, in fact, tended to shift local civil servants from place to place, perhaps in part to inhibit any strengthening of the aristocracy as an independent political force. If anything, this circulation of civil servants has increased in velocity since the establishment of the Republic.

inevitably, a man who smells of the market place, not of the palace. Again, one can see the strong and weak points of these two types of pattern so far as economic growth is concerned. The Modjokuto *homo economicus* pattern would seem to have a tendency to produce the kinds of attitudes supportive of democratic liberalism, of individual political freedom, and of intellectual autonomy which we regard as the chief goals of modernization, and as being in the long run more conducive to economic creativity and dynamism as such — as well as less dangerous to world peace — than a more state-centered, highly politicized, national, power-conscious approach. Yet there is a good deal of presumptive evidence that such a view of modernization as involving the rise of a free and independent bourgeoisie within a generally libertarian umpire state political framework is utopian in the context of the new states of Asia and Africa.[37] A purely business-based elite may be unable to cope with the scale of the modernization problem as such countries face it:

> Whereas in the West industrialism was built on centuries of slow accumulation of capital and techniques, the non-Western societies faced industrialism as an existent fact. They did not have to go through the slow process of accumulation which the West had, nor could they if they had wanted to. The capital required for modern industrialization was too great to be supplied by the existing economic mechanisms in these societies. What has happened is that in almost every case whatever industrialization has occurred has been government controlled or government-sponsored, because only the government has been able to marshal the requisite capital. Under these circumstances it is obvious that the strength of the polity and political values are crucial variables. . . . Whatever the specific form they take . . . political values and a strong polity would seem to be a great advantage and perhaps even a prerequisite for industrialization in the "backward" areas of today's world.[38]

[37] Of course, by "utopian" here is meant "unrealistic" not "ethically ideal." Other aspects of English type industrial revolutions — from urban blight to child labor — where state activity is limited to an umpire role are morally repellant to the modern mind.

[38] Bellah, *op. cit.*, pp. 192–93.

The *homo politicus* pattern of Tabanan would seem, therefore, rather closer to what appears to be functional to rapid economic expansion in late-developing "backward" nations. The Tabanan growth demonstrates in microcosm the dynamism which can occur when political motivations support economic innovation, when the entreprenurial and political elites tend to fuse. Although, as explained, much of the dynamism of the Tabanan nobles comes from a perceived threat to their political dominance, their economic activities are designed to maintain that dominance. In fact, far more than in Modjokuto there has been a close alliance between military and civil government and private businesses in Tabanan, until the latter have become quasi-public concerns, actual arms of government, as can be seen from the awarding of a coffee export monopoly to Gadarata, the canceling of the Chinese gasoline station license in order to allow Ksatria to operate the station, the close relations between the transport bureau which awards routes and the bus line *seka*, the obtaining of a tire-recapping monopoly by the Lord of Krambitan, and so on. In almost every case, the success of Tabanan's noble entrepreneurs has partly derived from their ability to gain or demand support from the local wing of the national government, and indeed, they have realized to a notable degree their aim of maintaining through economic means the substance of their local authority. The emergence, in Tabanan at least, of a unified elite of top civil servants and entrepreneurs, mainly under the aegis of the Nationalist Party, is fairly clear.[39]

The danger of such developments is, of course, that they are always skating fairly close to totalitarianism. Many of the more articulate and educated commoners in Tabanan do in fact regard the development in the past few years of an indigenous, upper-

[39] It must be remembered that, as noted, the nobility still dominates the civil service almost everywhere else in Bali. Even in Tabanan they have not been wholly displaced, and many of the newer civil servants are upper-caste individuals — Brahmanas, Vesias, etc. — who may be expected to have some community of outlook with the royal family. Thus, despite their sense of losing political control, the local aristocracy is far from having been wholly ousted and their economic efforts are in part supplementary to a continuing governmental role rather than entirely replacing political activity.

caste "big business" class as a genuinely ominous and discouraging occurrence and as a betrayal of the promises of the Revolution. It is always the same, they say: the people up on the hill get everything, the people down at the bottom get nothing; and it is upon such resentment that communism, just beginning to appear in Bali, feeds, though this sort of resentment is far from being confined to Communists. The development of a Japanese-type "industrial feudalism," a semitraditional, semimodern state capitalism, is a real possibility in a politically based developmental pattern, though it is a hardly necessary outcome of such a pattern. The placing of a traditional elite at the center of the process of economic modernization permits a more integral attack on the multiple problems this process creates than does the placing there of a foot-loose bourgeoisie, which must go at its task haphazardly and piecemeal; but it also encourages that intense domination of political concerns over all other concerns which is the hallmark of modernized totalitarian states.

Our final contrast is between the amount of urbanization which has occurred in the two towns. As noted above, on every index — from landholding to prostitution — Modjokuto is much more urbanized than Tabanan. Though Tabanan is several centuries older, it still has only begun to lose the solid outlines of a traditional court center, a cluster of villages surrounding a complex of palaces, while Modjokuto is well launched into that "advance toward vagueness" which characterizes modern urban life generally.

In general, urbanization has been held to be facilitative of economic growth. The familiar, more down-to-earth atmosphere, the free mingling of individuals from all walks of life, the greater personal anonymity and consequent protection from rigid moral constraints and prejudices, the more energetic, animated, variegated quality of everyday existence of the city and town as compared to the village have all been held stimulative to creativity in every field, including the economic. To a great extent, this invigorating, broadening, loosening quality of urban society is a fact, and such development as has occurred in Modjokuto is to a significant degree a reflex of the combination of an increased sense of possibility on the one hand and an intensely felt need to hustle for one's living on the other, characteristic of life in a town where the overwhelming majority of the population has no longer any immediate roots in traditional agrarian society. The brisk disorder of Modjokuto, compared to the sedate deliberateness of Tabanan, is on one level certainly conducive to change, flexibility, and aggressiveness, if only because it is impossible for anyone to stand still very long and continue to survive.

Yet urbanization, particularly when it occurs within a wider society which is economically stagnant, also breeds malaise, discouragement, and aimlessness. When the energies undoubtedly liberated by urban development find little productive outlet over an extended period of time, when the initial sense of opportunity proves to be psychologically rather than sociologically rooted, the result is an urban man who is restless rather than energetic, bewildered rather than confident, stranded rather than genuinely free. Lacking a truly dynamic core, life becomes makeshift in quality, gathers around it an air of exigency and insubstantiality, and though there is a great deal of hubbub, the over-all effect is one of agitated stability rather than of growth and change. Modjokuto's entrepreneurs, her one partially creative element, operate in a social context marked not by spirited innovation but by hectic and defensive expediency. Urbanization may or may not be a necessary condition for economic take-off; certainly it is not a sufficient condition.

Whether Tabanan, now begining its process of urbanization in the modern sense of the term, is in a better position is unclear. On the one hand, the lack of a large commercial class, a developed proletariat, and a strong office-clerk and schoolteacher intellectual group may hamper expansion, as may the greater provincialism and placidity of the town population in general. On the other hand, Tabanan may be fortunate in starting its whole process of modernization at a time when it may prove possible to avoid the sort of change without progress characteristic of Modjokuto since the middle thirties. Again, everything depends upon what happens in Indonesia as a whole, but if over the next decade or so economic opportunities do expand significantly, Tabanan's lack

of a history of boom, bust, and stagnation may prove advanta-
geous. Half an urbanization may be worse than none. There is
some basis for arguing that there exists an "optimal moment"
for making a rapid transition from traditionalism to modernism
just at that point where the old social structure begins to dissolve:
the society which (as Modjokuto perhaps did in the plantation
period) misses this opportunity and loses its customary form, while
at the same time being unable to realize fully a modern one, may
have been deprived of a valuable chance for smooth social transformation which will never come again, so that such transformation, though it seemingly must take place sooner or later, will
needs be slower and more painful.[40]

However this may be, it is clear that Tabanan's relatively lower
degree of urbanization has given her one clear advantage: she
has a far less serious "Chinese problem." As noted earlier, Chinese
merchants, operating under a crown-monopoly system, have been
trading in and around Tabanan for centuries. Yet Bali, unlike
Java, never reached a high degree of commercial development. It
lacked Java's great river plains, its excellent north coast ports, and
its massive population, and remained, throughout the Netherlands East Indies period, more or less a backwater so that the
bazaar economy never really took hold there with much force.
Even in this century, Bali has attracted little outside capital,
Dutch or Chinese (save, perhaps, in the tourist business, which
has never had any measurable effect on Tabanan), and the building up of a strong and aggressive Chinese business community controlling the main arteries of trade has been minimal. Not only
are the absolute numbers fewer — about 800 *vs.* about 2,000 — but
whereas in Modjokuto there is a large contingent of China-born
Chinese with but marginal involvement in Javanese culture
as such, in Tabanan almost the whole Chinese population is
Indonesian-born for several generations, relatively highly accultur-
ated to Balinese patterns, and much less intensely in opposition

[40] The discussion by Levy (M. J. Levy, "Contrasting Factors in the Modernization of China and Japan" in S. Kuznets *et al.* [eds.] *Economic Growth:
Brazil, India, Japan* [Durham, N.C.: Duke University Press, 1955]) of contrasting factors in Chinese and Japanese modernization implicitly lends support to this "if it were done, it were best done quickly" theory.

to their Balinese co-townsmen. And, as it is the China-born Chinese almost everywhere in Indonesia who are the most dynamic and aggressive businessmen, while the Indonesia-born are, commonly, much less vigorous and rather more nearly on a par with their Indonesian opposite numbers in commercial matters, Tabanan's aristocratic-entrepreneur faces nothing even resembling the entrenched, resourceful, and bitterly antagonistic Chinese business community with which Modjokuto's former peddlers must contend.

Before the war the few stores and small factories in Tabanan were, indeed, exclusively Chinese owned. Unlike Modjokuto, Tabanan had no "indigenous" businessmen at all, and as what bazaar activity there was, was dominated, as explained earlier, by non-Balinese Indonesians, Balinese involvement in interlocal commerce was marginal at best. Lacking the general economic evolution which Modjokuto experienced in the interwar years, Tabanan by 1950 had neither a precariously established "indigenous" entrepreneurial group nor an aggressive Chinese community, so that when the young aristocrats moved in to take over the unrealized opportunities for economic expansion, they had less difficulty in overcoming any similar move on the part of the Chinese.[41] Although the role of the Chinese in the local economy is important, and at least one case of genuine entreprenurial expansion is evident in the person of the owner of a motion-picture theater, soft-drink bottling works, and cigarette factory, the Chinese as a whole do not seem to be such a major obstacle to the Balinese entrepreneurs as they are to the Javanese.

In sum, we have a fairly sharp contrast between the two sorts of developmental process. On the one hand, we have the crystalliza-

[41] The weaker, functionally less crucial position of the Chinese has also meant that the civil government and the military move against them more easily. Although the intensity of the feeling between the Chinese and Javanese is very much greater — nothing like the Modjokuto atrocities of the Revolution occurred in Tabanan — the repression of the Chinese has been much more effective in Bali than in Java, where they are too deeply entrenched in the economy to be tampered with with impunity. (This will not, of course, necessarily protect them forever; the importance of the Dutch to the effective functioning of Indonesia's economy did not prevent their near-total displacement in December, 1957.)

tion of a genuine small-businessman class of shopkeepers and manufacturers out of a general bazaar-trading background. Religious
nonconformists, individualists, economically minded, and very
little bound by the constraints of traditional village society so far
as business is concerned, these all-too-classical self-made entrepreneurs are hampered mainly by their inability to form stable, large-
scale firms and by the general dispiritedness of a society in which
the loosening effects of urbanization have proceeded more rapidly
than the reconstructive ones. On the other hand, we have the emergence out of a declining agrarian oligarchy of a politically based
and motivated elite of renovated aristocrats. Strengthened by their
ability to mobilize the loyalties of traditional society for novel
ends, these rather grander entrepreneurs, more reminiscent, perhaps, of Japan than of England, are hindered by the difficulty of
freeing specifically economic concerns from diffusely cultural ones
and by the tendency of political interests to dominate and even
swallow up all others. In Modjokuto, one finds a liberation of
business activities from the normative constraints of peasant society, combined with a relative lack of effective collective organization of them; in Tabanan, one finds the employment of customary
organizational forms in modern economic pursuits, combined
with a relative inability to divest these forms of their traditional,
non-economic social and cultural implications.

Yet, from one point of view, the problems faced by Modjokuto
and Tabanan entrepreneurial groups are fundamentally very similar. Sociologically speaking, perhaps the major difference between
a modern economy and a traditional one is that the former is
marked by a very large number of social structures, institutions,
and roles specifically adapted to fulfil economic functions as opposed to others, while for the most part the latter is not: a modern
economy is, in the jargon, more differentiated. The firm is an
excellent sociological benchmark of development, at least in the
initial phases, precisely because it is just such a specifically economic institution, a miniature social system specialized to perform
economic functions and integrated in terms of economic values.
And it is such firms that the entrepreneurs of both Modjokuto and
Tabanan are trying to create.

But the construction of a viable firm in a pretake-off country such as Indonesia requires two very difficult and somewhat contradictory achievements: a sufficient degree of independence of the — from an economic point of view — non-rational pressures of institutionalized custom, and the establishment of an accepted normative code in terms of which completely economic activities may be regulated. Without the first, business firms sink into the inefficiency with which those of Tabanan are usually threatened; without the second they flounder on the shoals of mistrust, as Modjokuto's tend to do.

The two achievements are somewhat contradictory because the more a firm (and a firm economy) is based on a strictly rational economic basis in a still semitraditional society, the more difficult it is to regulate it in terms of the customary moral values of the society as a whole. A modern economy demands not only differentiated social institutions for its effective functioning, but a specialized ethical code attuned to the requirements of business, itself only a particular version of the basic value system of the whole society. This code performs the crucial functions of defining the boundaries within which the free play of economic rationality is permitted and of stabilizing the relation of economic to non-economic pursuits within the over-all culture. In these terms, economic development involves the establishment of a well-demarcated preserve within which economic rationality may operate independently of political, religious, familial, and other interests, as well as a definition of the place and value of such businesslike behavior from the point of view of the total social system, the manner in which, even within its own preserve, it too must submit to regulation by the culture's general moral code. In modern society the range within which economic rationality is allowed to hold sway is generally wide and the control of more general normative concerns at least somewhat loose, but in any case the range has definite limits and the control is quite real. It is the attempt to achieve this reconciliation of a broader field for the operation of purely economic calculation with the maintenance of normative control in economic matters with which the entrepreneurs of our two towns are, at base, concerned.

A bazaar economy provides a preserve for the exercise of economic rationality independently of non-economic constraints, but it does so by means of a nearly total insulation of commercial behavior from the general nexus of cultural activities. Trading is set apart, compartmentalized; it develops as an interstitial pursuit, one to which the values of the wider society are by common agreement held not to apply, and the disruptive qualities of this agreement are minimized through the process of sharp social and cultural segregation of both traders and trading. As noted, the bazaar economy, in such a situation, necessarily develops a specific ethic of its own, for no ordered social activity can proceed without normative control. But the ethic thus evolved is so precisely adjusted to person-to-person, higgling and haggling, credit-balance peddling that it is largely inadequate for the regulation of the more collectively and systematically organized world of the firm, where simple compartmentalization is, in any case, no longer a workable solution of the problem of the integration of economic with non-economic social processes. Modjokuto entrepreneurs, as a result, have experienced few difficulties with the first of our two general sociological prerequisites for growth: the achievement of a sufficient degree of independence for economic activity from the (economically) non-rational pressure of institutionalized custom; they have not been much shackled by peasant society traditionalism. But they are, so far, stymied by the second; the establishment of an accepted and workable normative code, in terms of which complexly organized economic activities can be regulated and integrated into the general society. Bazaar economy egoism still hangs heavily over them.

Tabanan's entrepreneurs, on the other hand, have met the second problem fairly effectively but have experienced relatively severe difficulties with the first. Balinese peasant society is, as we have seen, a reservoir of organizational forms, all more or less modeled on the *seka* principle, which, especially when combined with traditional political loyalties, can be fairly effectively applied to the construction of firms. The ingrained Balinese tendency to tailor collective social groups to fairly specific ends, including in some cases even narrowly economic ones, and their custom-rooted willingness to follow the lead of the indigenous aristocracy in supra-village matters are both traits of positive functional value in the creation of at least semimodern business concerns. Traditional peasant society social structures, far from inevitably acting as barriers and hindrances to economic change may, if they are the right sort of structures in the right sort of situation, actually facilitate it. Nevertheless, the associated normative implications of these structures, radical egalitarian collectivism on the one hand and political oligarchy on the other, tend to interfere with the free play of economic rationality and to form serious obstacles to further growth, particularly as the secondary changes in the general society induced by economic innovations begin to appear.

Despite their important differencees, therefore, the economic innovators of Modjokuto and Tabanan find themselves today in a very similar position. Seizing upon the elements of pre-Revolutionary society most facilitative of economic modernization, they have propelled themselves well into that no man's land of transition which lies between a peasant society past and an industrial society future. Capitalizing on the bazaar economy's business-is-business orientation, a few of Modjokuto's shrewder traders have begun to create genuine, functionally specific, commercial and industrial firms; drawing upon the "duck-like" collectivism of the Balinese village and upon their own oligarchic traditions, some of Tabanan's more dynamic aristocrats have initiated a fundamental reorganization of the town's whole economic system. But now that the two groups have emerged into the strangely landscaped and ill-defined zone where neither the forms of ancient custom nor those of the modern West offer reliable guides to action, they are gradually coming to discover that these readjusted older patterns are insufficient to complete the task which they have set themselves: Modjokuto's firms fail to grow, Tabanan's fail to rationalize. For the first phases of development, renovation is perhaps enough, but for the succeeding ones thorough reconstruction is demanded. The mentalities of the peddler and the prince must both be abandoned, and in their place must come that of the professional manager; for the temporary props of the usable past must be substituted the permanent foundations of a differentiated economic ethic which both justifies economic rationality and provides it with a moral framework which gives it more than an individual, social, referent. But, as for both groups reconstruction implies the abandonment of those very attitudes, beliefs, and values which have made their initial successes possible — stubborn self-reliance on the one hand, imperious assumption of intrinsic superiority on the other — it is extremely difficult to estimate which of them will find such fundamental change easier, or when either will be able to accomplish it.

Conclusion: Modjokuto, Tabanan, And Indonesia

Indonesia as a nation is not the village or the small town writ large. It is an autonomous social system with its own proper characteristics, its own dynamics, its own purposes and problems. One cannot, therefore, generalize in any direct way from a Modjokuto or a Tabanan to the country as a whole. To do so is to commit the fallacy of composition in an egregious manner; it is to confuse the elements of a synthesis with the synthesis itself.

What, then, is the relevance of such detailed studies of specific and circumscribed subsocieties as the two here presented for an assessment of Indonesia's developmental prospect in general? What can we learn from a careful analysis of the socioeconomic patterns and processes of Modjokuto and Tabanan about those of the nation of which they are a part? In what ways is the anthropologist's characteristic approach to the problem of economic growth related to that which the economist usually employs?

In the main, the value of systematic studies of particular communities for the understanding of national economic development lies (1) in their more intensive probing of particular dynamics which are, nevertheless, of broader general significance; and (2) in their more circumstantial depiction of the nature of the social and cultural context within which development inevitably will have to take place. A Tabanan or a Modjokuto provides on the one hand a particular setting within which some of the more fundamental processes of economic modernization as such can be seen in a specific and determinate form, and, on the other, a concrete example of the kind of parametric social conditions with which over-all policies and programs, no matter how ambitious or how comprehensively stated, must in the long run come to grips. Anthropological studies add depth and realism to the more abstract and formal analyses characteristic of aggregative economics.

Social Dynamics of Economic Modernization

So far as dynamics are concerned, the material presented above brings what is perhaps the central problem in this whole area — how fundamental a social and cultural transformation does economic modernization demand? — into sharp focus. Most recent writers have stressed the totality, the thoroughgoing nature of the change involved in the transition to sustained economic growth. Modernized industrial societies tend to take a form specific and peculiar to them. They come to resemble one another more and more closely as they develop, not merely in their economic functioning but in their type of value system, their sort of class structure, their pattern of government, even in their family organization and their religious beliefs.[1] The relation of what occurs in one part of a social system to what happens in another, the necessary functional interdependencies in any such system, is stressed here: industrialism may not necessarily involve free-enterprise capitalism, but it does involve the decline of magic, the construction of a universal legal and moral code, increased social mobility, the bureaucratization of government, and the isolation of the elementary family from strong extended kinship ties. The total, system-wide conception of change involved in this sort of analysis is implicit in the dichotomous typological terms it seems inevitably to invoke: *gemeinschaft* vs. *gesellschaft*; tradi-

[1] For this view see T. Parsons, *The Social System* (Glencoe, Ill.: Free Press, 1951), pp. 182–91. The original source of this position is, of course, Max Weber's concept of "rationalization."

tional *vs.* modern; folk vs. urban; universalistic-specific *vs.* particularistic-diffuse — and so on.

At the same time, some recent analyses have stressed the fact that a great deal of economic development, in the technical sense of increased per capita productivity, can take place within a context of general social and cultural conservatism in which essentially traditional values and social structures are so adapted as to be capable of integration with more efficient economic practices. Japan, whose economic system is still to a great extent organized in terms of concepts of personal loyalty and social status directly derivative from traditional political organization, is a prime example; but the commercial and industrial activities of the Chinese of Singapore, Hong Kong, and (pre-Communist) Shanghai indicate that fairly high levels of economic efficiency can be achieved on the basis of a bazaar economy ethic as well.[2] To some extent at least, such studies suggest that the impact of economic modernization upon the total social system is not necessarily as revolutionary and all-embracing as it has sometimes been described; or, put somewhat differently, a modern economic system may be compatible with a wider range of non-economic cultural patterns and social structures than has often been thought.[3]

The issue, properly stated however, is, not whether each and

[2] On Japan see James G. Abegglen, *The Japanese Factory: Aspects of Its Social Organization* (Glencoe, Ill.: Free Press, 1958). Studies of developed bazaar economies are wanting, but for an example of such an economy rather more advanced than Modjokuto's see Ju-Kang T'ien, *The Chinese of Sarawak*, Monographs on Social Anthropology, No. 12 (London: London School of Economics and Political Science, n.d.).

[3] For Indonesia, all this takes on more practical significance, because almost the whole of the indigenous intellectual elite, regardless of political allegiance, is ideologically committed both to the industrialization of the country and to an avoidance of what it regards as the morally and aesthetically repugnant aspects of the advanced industrial societies now in existence. The members of this elite wish to create a fully rationalized economy without most of the broader cultural concomitants which have characterized that sort of economy in the West. Without some such belief — or a cynical concentration on the simple expansion of national power — it is doubtful that the motivational commitment of the members of the local intelligentsia to radical economic reform could be maintained. The notion that American culture is an indissoluble correlate of American productive technique is a wholly unacceptable one to the leadership in the majority of Asian countries.

every aspect of society must change or nothing but the economy itself must change in the process of economic rationalization; for clearly neither of these extreme positions is defensible. Rather it is: What must change and what need not? And even to this question there is, as yet, no single, wholly general answer, for much depends upon precisely the sort of traditional system from which one is departing and the sort of modern system one is attempting to create. The Weberian tradition is without doubt correct in insisting that economic change is inevitably part and parcel of broader changes occurring throughout society, not an isolated and independent sequence of events. Where it is less certainly correct is in assuming an essential uniformity of the relationship between economic and non-economic changes from case to case. From a narrowly economic point of view development takes the same general form always and everywhere; it consists of a progressively more rational employment of scarce means toward the achievement of specified material ends. But from a sociological point of view it is not clear that such a basic and obvious similiarity of form exists, that the changes in religious outlook, class structure, family organization, and so on are identical from one developing society to another. In any case, the employment of highly generalized dichotomous concepts, of holistic types, to describe these broader processes, in the light of our still confused and uncertain understanding of them and of their interrelations with the much better conceptualized processes of economic rationalization, would seem premature. It obscures the very differences we want to investigate in the hope of eventually arriving at some more solidly founded general regularities.

It is in this regard that studies such as those of Modjokuto and Tabanan become relevant to more general theoretical issues. In essence, the process of development in the narrowly economic sense is identical, or nearly so, in the two cases. It consists, as we have noted, first of the clearing of a broader field for the free play of economic rationality, and, second, of the construction of a specific normative code, an economic ethic, in terms of which this rationality can be socially regulated. But the sorts of reorganizations, readjustments, reforms, and reconstructions which must take place in the wider society to permit and facilitate the evolution of such a rationalized economy, and, hence, the manner in which that economy is fitted, as it develops, into the broader society, differs quite sharply between the Javanese town and the Balinese. An ambitious shopkeeper class, urban homogenization, Islamic reform, a proliferation of quasi-political nationalist organizations, and intense minority-group problems on the one side give a quite different picture than an uneasy aristocracy, religious conservatism, a fusion of political and economic elites, "pluralistic collectivism," and the confinement of business activities to a small percentage of the population give on the other. Both towns, in a broad sense of the term, may be "traditionalistic," but they represent different sorts of traditionalism. Similarly, both will presumably become "modern" when economic growth really takes hold, but it seems likely that they will then show contrasting sorts of modernity.

The description and analysis of such developing, but pretake-off towns as Modjokuto and Tabanan thus enable us to get behind the gross dichotomous and over-systematic ideal types which have customarily been employed in this field, and to introduce a greater flexibility into our notions of what sort of economic structures are compatible with what sort of non-economic ones within a given social system. Comparing the bazaar, trade-based pattern of Modjokuto with the court, politically based pattern of Tabanan brings home to us the range of variation possible in the developmental process as a whole, whatever the properly economic uniformities involved may be. And, by providing us with a more realistic and differentiated typology, such comparisons should enable us to state generalizations about development as a social and cultural process in far more concrete and circumstantial terms than is permitted us by the simple assumption of a *pari passu* increase of rationality in all aspects of social life.

Nor must such a procedure necessarily lead to the sort of atheoretical, "every case is different" indeterminateness for which anthropologists are, unfortunately, so notorious. The range of sociocultural variation in the developmental process is as far from being infinite as it is from being non-existent. Not everything is possible: some interrelationships between economic and non-economic processes are more nearly invariant than others, and there are, we must suppose, genuine regularities of social and cultural change which are associated with economic rationalization generally. But it is only through an extended series of intensive comparative investigations of different varieties of developmental process that we can achieve the conceptual isolation of such regularities, and so break out of the *gemeinschaft* to *gesellschaft* sort of thinking which, whatever its general uses, now so hampers the creation of a workable "middle range" sociological theory of economic growth.

What specific sociological generalizations about the dynamics of development, then, can we hazard on the basis of the limited, two-case comparative analysis here conducted? We shall set forth six propositions concerning the nature of pretake-off social change which the Modjokuto and Tabanan material suggest. Clearly such propositions must be treated as only tentative hypotheses, derived as they are from a single comparison.[4] Whether or how far they will stand up when tested against the great number of community studies which need to be done before we can speak with any assurance about these matters simply remains to be seen.

1. *Innovative economic leadership (entrepreneurship)
occurs in a fairly well defined and socially
homogeneous group.*

There is, on a priori grounds, no reason why the entrepreneurs of Modjokuto and Tabanan could not come either randomly from the general population or from several distinct social groups at once. But in fact they do not. Rather, in both cases, they come almost entirely from a single quite clearly demarcated group, somewhat set apart: the pious Islamic traders in Modjokuto, the

---

[4] To a great extent, of course, they are derived as well from theoretical preconceptions based on a knowledge both of the relevant social science literature and on a general familiarity with the developmental processes in Indonesia, the underdeveloped world, and the premodern West generally. They are not wholly inductive.

ruling family in Tabanan. In both towns there are a few exceptions to this rule — a few more in Modjokuto than in Tabanan
— but in the main the core of economic leadership is socially
highly homogeneous in terms of class standings, religious outlook,
occupational background, political affiliation, etc., so that one
can speak quite realistically of a definite entrepreneurial group
within the general society. In both towns, too, the existence of
such a specialized group is, at least among the entrepreneurs
themselves, and to a great extent among the mass of the people,
quite consciously apprehended.

> 2. *This innovative group has crystallized out of a
> larger traditional group which has a very long
> history of extra-village status and interlocal
> orientation.*

Although, particularly in Bali, a good deal of economic enterprise is found among the peasantry, both entrepreneurial groups
stand outside the immediate purview of village social structure,
as did the traditional groups from which they have emerged.
Further, both groups are primarily interlocal in their outlook,
some of their most important ties being with groups and individuals in areas other than their own, and this too is a heritage
from their progenitors. In Modjokuto, this "horizontal" orientation was originally a correlate of the all-Indonesia trading network
which grew out of the internationally based bazaar culture of the
fifteenth and sixteenth centuries. The entrepreneurs are sons and
grandsons of men who came there originally as itinerant, market-
circuit traders, mostly from the polyglot north coastal areas where
the bazaar culture first flourished in the string of harbor towns
lining the Java Sea. These mobile and worldly-wise merchants
had commercial ties, if petty and fluctuating ones, extending over
a great part of small-town Java, and their successors maintain a
similar pattern today. In Tabanan, horizontality grew out of the
sophisticated court culture associated with the indigenous Indo-
nesion state structure, which found its climax in the great medieval
empire of Madjapahit and of which Bali's kingdoms were an in-

tegral part. Tabanan's aristocracy not only formed a regional ruling group, but had and still has important and intimate social relationships with similar groups in the other regional capitals of the island. In both cases, the heirs of a long tradition of levantine or patrician cosmopolitanism, insulated by occupation or by rank from the localized bonds of village society have formed the vanguard of economic change.[5]

3. *The larger group out of which the innovative group is emerging is one which is at present experiencing a fairly radical change in its relationships with the wider society of which it is a part.*

Within prewar Modjokuto society the town's traders were a self-contained, rather despised minority group; today they are becoming integrated into a broad and generalized middle class within an uncertainly urbanizing structure. In prewar Tabanan society, the aristocrats formed the unquestioned political and cultural elite of the entire region; today their position is increasingly threatened by the growth of a universal civil bureaucracy and the populist sentiments of nationalist ideology. In both cases, economic innovation seems in part to be a response to the status insecurity engendered by these shifts in social structure.[6] It has been a relatively sudden altering of what for these groups were considered fixed co-ordinates of social and cultural existence

[5] One of the interesting questions this study raises, but, because of the weakness of the state tradition in Modjokuto and of the bazaar tradition in Tabanan, cannot answer, is what occurs when both of these are found in vigorous form in the same town. Cursory knowledge of the small Javanese city of Jogjakarta, where this occurs, suggests that entrepreneurial groups may then emerge from both of these horizontal traditions, leading to a much more complex dynamic picture than that found in either of our towns.

[6] Of course, from a broader point of view the essential theoretical question here is why the dominant response to strain in both these cases has been mainly "positive" and "constructive," rather than "irrational," "retreatist," or "rebellious." To some extent, the more negative reactions are also found among certain members of these dislocated groups, but a description of them would take us too far afield, and in both towns they have not so far been of much significance. With continued stagnation on the national level they might, however, become more important.

which has projected some of their members into the area of economic innovation. It is neither upward nor downward class mobility, nor a blockage of these which is necessarily crucial; but rather a decisive change in intergroup relations of any sort, which by throwing accepted status demarcations into disarray stimulated active efforts to anchor social positions to new moorings.

4. *On the ideological level the innovative group conceives of itself as the main vehicle of religious and moral excellence within a generally wayward, unenlightened, or heedless community.*

In Modjokuto, Islamic reform, a sort of Moslem puritanism, is the doctrine of the overwhelming majority of the entrepreneurs. This ideology aims at a radical purification of the prevailing religious and moral syncretism of heterodox elements, and is intensely critical of a wide range of established usages in the fields of ethics and worship. Always the creed of a numerically relatively small group, Islamic Reform has demanded of its followers a more rigorous, more intense, and purer adherence to what it regards as "the true spirit of the Koran and the Hadith" than it takes to be at all common among the mass of the people, as well as a constant and unremitting educational and propaganda effort to close the gap between the genuinely enlightened few and the semipagan many.

The ideology of Tabanan's new men, on the other hand, is neither puritan nor reformative; rather it is catholic and restorationist. But there is the same sense of representing the proper against the prevailing. The increasing abandonment of customary patterns of deference, the progressive usurpation of political power by the hereditarily unequipped, and the growing failure on the part of the average man to recognize and appreciate the onerous yet indispensable social and cultural functions performed by those of high status for the community as a whole — all these are taken to be signs of a general cultural decline against which it is the aristocracy's inherited duty to continue to stand as exemplars of the genuinely valuable. Such a view could easily

lead to a dispirited and bitter feeling that the world is passing
one by, as it has among Modjokuto's much smaller and weaker
gentry class; but among the still self-confident and powerful
Tabanan aristocracy it has led to a vigorous attempt to support
a traditional cynosure role on other grounds. In any case, both
innovative groups tend to see the general cultural level of the
whole wider community as almost entirely dependent upon the
success of themselves and their activities.

5. *The major innovations and innovational problems the*
entrepreneurs face are organizational rather
than technical.

At the present stage of development, the innovators of neither
town are primarily concerned with technical problems; neither of
these small-scale economic revolutions focuses around the inventor, the engineer, or even the craftsman. In great part this is
true because most of the specifically technical problems have
already been solved and one need only adapt them to local needs:
an Indonesian entrepreneur does not have to invent a sugar press,
an ice machine, or a tire-recapper — he has only to purchase them.
Although some individuals — particularly in Modjokuto — often
show a great deal of technical ingenuity in constructing composite machines or in keeping old and outdated ones performing,
the mentality of the tinkerer, of the Henry Ford type of self-taught
inventor and engineer, a Tom Swift "putting dirigibles together
out in the backyard," is largely lacking in the innovative groups
of both towns. Superior mechanical aptitude, imagination, or
knowledge is not a characteristic which sets entrepreneurs apart
from non-entrepreneurs, or successful entrepreneurs from unsuc-
cessful ones in present-day Modjokuto or Tabanan.

The prerequisite for success is rather organizational and administrative skill. To a certain extent this is more obvious in
Tabanan than Modjokuto, but even in the Javanese town the
qualifications needed to set up a factory primarily involve skills
concerned with the mobilization of existing social and economic
resources, the organization of a group of largely undisciplined

workers into a co-ordinated, persistent, productive effort, and a systematic administration of both the manufacturing and marketing ends of the business. It is not the technically most skilled carpenter or tailor who becomes the manager of a sawmill contracting firm or a garment factory, but the most skilled handler of men. In Tabanan, this is even clearer: with the exception of the garage mechanic bus-line director (whose main contribution to the formation of the line was organizational rather than technical), none of the important noble entrepreneurs seems to have any particular mechanical flair whatever.

The fact that much developmental advance in these towns at the moment involves a restructuring and simplification of the distributive apparatus also strengthens the hand of the organizer over that of the engineer, and makes the ability to give effective social form to rationalized economic activities the fundamental requisite of a successful entrepreneur. This all may change somewhat as development accelerates; but it seems likely that the engineer-inventor will not play the central role in stimulating Indonesian take-off that he did in England and America.

6. *The function of the entrepreneur in such transitional but pretake-off societies is mainly to adapt customarily established means to novel ends.*

The economic innovators of Modjokuto and Tabanan are Janus-like: halfway between the past and the future, they face in both directions. It is in their ability to operate at once in the traditional world of established custom and in the modern world of systematic economic rationality which is their chief resource. In Modjokuto, the small shopkeepers and manufacturers capitalize on the knowledge and skills developed within the bazaar economy and attempt to apply them toward the creation of economic institutions more complex and more efficient than the bazaar economy has so far been able to produce. In Tabanan, the businessmen nobles redirect the political loyalties of agrarian society into the support of economic rationalization. Both groups draw much of their strength from this ability to operate on both sides of the line between traditional and modern in economic matters and so form a bridge between the two. As a result, they are able to create transitional economic institutions within which many of the values, structures, beliefs, and skills of a customary trading or peasant culture are integrated with features characteristic of developed and specialized firm economies.

As noted, probably they will eventually have to purge these institutions — and themselves — of most of these more antique props to innovative activities and rest their economic leadership on more technical economic bases. But in the meantime their half-modern, half-traditional approach to entrepreneurship represents the towns' furthest advance toward the initiation of sustained economic growth.

Local Development and National Planning

Aside from their more intensive probing of some of the more fundamental sociological and anthropological dynamics of development, systematic studies of particular communities also portray the variability of the specific settings within which these dynamics are actually expressed. They not only isolate some of the common factors and constants of development, but they also demonstrate the variety of forms which growth, as a unified process, can take. A longer series of Indonesian cases, if ever we have one, should lead both to a deeper understanding of development as a generalized, abstract process and a more profound appreciation of the tremendous diversity of concrete social and cultural contexts within which that generalized process can be imbedded. Such studies instil in us a sense not just of inevitability but of possibility; and even Modjokuto and Tabanan demonstrate quite clearly that there is no one invariable road to take-off.

From the point of view of Indonesian development as a whole, this suggests that national planning ought not to proceed, as it commonly does, on the assumption that take-off either demands or will automatically bring in its wake a uniform series of social changes throughout the whole of the country. Changes, and fundamental ones, it will clearly bring; but what sorts of changes they will be is dependent both upon the precise sort of traditional structures which already exist and the precise sort of economic innovations which take-off turns out actually to involve. Because economic rationalization can occur within a wide variety of cultural contexts, because the specific, non-economic prerequisites for it differ from one such context to the next (so that such often-asked general questions as "Is the joint family facilitative or inhibitory of economic growth?" are really meaningless), and because it does not inevitably create any one sort of social environment, over-all developmental policies need to be much more delicately attuned to the particularities of local social and cultural organization than they have been so far.

This is especially necessary in a country with the unusually variegated geography, history, and ethnic composition of Indonesia. Her archipelagic existence has always enforced upon her an extreme degree of cultural heterogeneity, and, located as she is at the crossroads of the Orient, she has been subjected to a continual series of in themselves incompatible religious, economic, and political influences — Indians, Arabs, Chinese, Portuguese, Dutch, English have all passed through with their doctrines, their ambitions, and their skills. And her proper genius has, consequently, always lain in her ability to work out practicable adjustments among her constituent cultures and to absorb the great host of external influences impinging upon her while still, somehow, maintaining a distinct and over-all unique character. No great continental power with a large core area of relatively uniform, classically standardized culture — a China, an India, or a Russia — not even a homogeneous and out-of-the-way island nation like Japan, Indonesia has continually been forced to create and re-create an only partly realized synthesis of a very wide range of different cultural traditions, social structures, and psychological types. As a nation it has always consisted of a mélange of elements: of rice-growing peasants, cattle-herders, jungle hunters, open-sea fishermen, and sago and coconut horticulturalists; of Moslems, Hindus, Buddhists, Christians, cannibals, head-hunters, and Melanesian pig and gong fanciers; of far-flung market systems, elaborate patrimonial bureaucracies, settled peasant villages, capital-intensive plantations, and wandering slash-and-burn tribes. Indonesia's true national tradition is not simple but compound, not unitary, but multiple, not systematic but irregular. And her greatest periods have not been those in which some fundamental classical tradition has emerged and in pure form dominated the whole but those, such as the Madjapahit, in which the whole great heterogeneity of contemporary culture came into some loose and flexible over-all framework of integration through which it could find a direct and complete expression in all its variety of detail.

The ideologies of modern nationalism, on the other hand, arising as they do out of an intense concern with massive social reconstruction, show a strong tendency toward a neglect, even an outright denial, of important variations in domestic cultural patterns and of internal social discontinuities. The vivid memory on the part of the elites of the New States of colonial divide-and-rule policies, as well as a fear of the strong divisive tendencies they quite accurately perceive both within themselves and in the mass of the population, leads them to regard any explicit and frank concern with internal diversity as subversive of the whole nation-building effort and to view, or try to view, their own society in a much too uniform and global, even stereotypic a manner. With regard to national economic planning this leads to a failure to cast proposals in a form which attempts to take maximum advantage of the peculiarities of various local traditions, to an unwillingness even to consider differentiated plans for different cultural and social groups, and to a form of programming which, rather than searching for specific growing points within the domestic economy and precisely tailoring efforts with respect to them, develops an a priori schedule of priorities based on external or abstract theoretical considerations. In Indonesia, such an approach goes wholly against the grain of the natural character and pattern of growth of the country and, rather than creating unity, accentuates the conflicts already present. In the overconcern with national integration, conceived in a wholly monistic sense, the very construction of such integration, which, unless it is to be totalitarian must rest on a pluralistic basis, may be undermined. All this is not to say that Indonesia does not badly need centralized planning or firm direction from a self-conscious, Western-educated national elite. The entire momentum necessary for a transition to sustained growth is not likely to come "from below"; it will not arise spontaneously out of the dislocations and re-equilibrations of modern village and small-town life, no matter how intense they may become. It is romanticism or worse to suppose that the large-scale mobilization of human and natural resources needed for take-off can occur on a piecemeal, unco-ordinated, laissez faire basis: a 2 per cent per annum population rise in a country where per capita income is probably already falling makes this clear enough. To urge this sort of "grass-roots and small-industry" policy on Indonesia, whether in the name of libertarianism or on the basis of a sentimental regard for the vitality of local enterprise, is to condemn her to wander in the no man's land of transition indefinitely.

But to say that Indonesian development must in great part be consciously planned is not to say that such planning should take place in deliberate ignorance of the very domestic social and cultural processes which it is supposedly concerned to transform. To say that many of the basic developmental decisions must be made centrally is not to say they should be made without regard to local developments or that the exact nature of these develop-ments should have no effect upon them. And to say that the entire dynamic basis for Indonesian take-off cannot come from below is not to say that such a dynamic can be created by government fiat and without capitalizing on the wide variety of innovational forces already at work in the society generally. For successful developmental planning within an at least partially democratic framework it is necessary that programs and policies be designed to encourage, support, and intensify processes of economic ration-alization such as those described for Modjokuto and Tabanan as they appear throughout the whole of the country, and that government-sponsored enterprise be keyed in with that arising autochthonously in the general population. Such planning im-plies a break with a global, monistic, hypernational approach and a shift to a pluralistic one differentiated in terms of the tremendous differences in the way in which the problem of development presents itself from class to class, from town to town, and from region to region. Such a shift implies a search for specific growing points rather than a scattershot crash-program, a tolerance for discontinuities in levels of development from place to place and sector to sector rather than a steadfast commitment to the Utopia of balanced growth, and a complication of the formal elegance of economic theory with the irregularities and imponderables of social process. It implies pragmatism, concreteness, and realism; and a willingness to use general principles, economic or sociological, not as axioms from which policies are to be logically deduced but as guides to the interpretation of particular cases upon which policies are to be based. In this sort of planning, anthropological studies are relevant not simply to an underbudgeted, relief-oriented "community development program," but to the whole range of developmental issues from import policy and taxation to industrial location and the allocation of scarce resources, for they describe the dimensions of the sociocultural world within which these issues take on a determinate and hence resolvable form.

Index

Printed and bound by CPI Group (UK) Ltd, Croydon, CR0 4YY

09/06/2025

14685697-0001